# THE PERCUSSIONIST'S DICTIONARY

Translations, Descriptions and Photographs of Percussion Instruments from Around the World

Compiled and Edited by
Joseph Adato and George Judy

SB-1040

A native of New York City, Joseph Adato attended Music and Art High School, the Juilliard School of Music where he received a Bachelor of Music, and Columbia University where he obtained a Masters Degree in Music Education. While a student at Juilliard, Mr. Adato studied percussion methods with Morris Goldenberg and timpani with Saul Goodman. Mr. Adato also spent several years of vibraphone studies with Phil Kraus.

While living in New York City, Mr. Adato performed with the New York Philharmonic, City Center Ballet Orchestra (New York State Ballet), Symphony of the Air (N.B.C. Symphony) and for many Broadway shows.

Mr. Adato joined the Cleveland Orchestra in 1962 as a member of the percussion section, a position he still holds. While living in Cleveland, Mr. Adato taught at Baldwin Wallace College 1963-1970, Akron University 1970-1978, and is currently Instructor of Percussion at Cleveland State University, a position he held since 1978.

George Judy, a native of Cleveland, Ohio, has studied drum-set locally with Edward Bobick and Bob McKee. Upon graduation from high school, Mr. Judy attended Cleveland State University where he studied percussion methods with Joseph Adato and Donald Miller. There he received his Bachelor of Arts in Music Performance and Education.

While at Cleveland State University, Mr. Judy began his professional career by performing with such personalities as Paul Anka, Jack Jones, Juliet Prowse, Shields and Yarnell, Mitzi Gaynor, Gladys Knight, Engelbert Humperdinck, Dinah Shore, Joel Grey, Harry Belafonte and more. A year before graduation Mr. Judy took a leave of absence to go on a national tour with the Broadway show "Oklahoma!". Mr. Judy has also performed with the Cleveland Orchestra, Cleveland Chamber Orchestra, Cleveland Philharmonic, Ohio Ballet Orchestra, and The Northcoast Percussion Ensemble.

In addition to his performing, Mr. Judy is a percussion instructor in the Cleveland area.

# PREFACE

All too often, percussionists, while practicing their trade, have been stymied by their inability to translate foreign percussion terminology into English, or by their inability to understand what kind of percussion instrument the composer has called for in his composition.

Up until now, percussionists have had to search through several references in order to "maybe" find the translation of those terms, and description of those percussion instruments, that they were looking for. We realize that this dictionary, as extensive as it is, does not contain every percussion instrument or term in existence, but only those that are commonly "heard" of or "used" in Western music. However, it is our hope that, with this publication, the search will be made easier.

To assist the reader, this dictionary has been divided into three sections. Section 1 contains an alphabetical listing of instruments, in English, with a short description of each instrument. Section 2 contains photographs of those instruments which the authors felt necessary to aid the descriptions found in Section 1. Section 3 contains all foreign terms and their translations. In this section we have indicated, as applicable, the country of origin, native term or the actual language of the instrument listed.

The following abbreviations that are found in Section 3 are as follows:

| | |
|---|---|
| Afr. - African | L. Amer. - Latin American |
| Braz. - Brazilian | Mex. - Mexican |
| C.A. - Central American | Mex. Ind. - Mexican Indian |
| Col. - Colombian | Or. - Oriental |
| Dan. - Danish | Pol. - Polish |
| Fr. - French | Port. - Portuguese |
| Ger. - German | Rus. - Russian |
| Gr. - Greek | S.A.I. - South American Indian |
| Guat. - Guatemalan | Sant. Dom. - Santo Domingo |
| Ind. - Indian | S. Amer. - South American |
| It. - Italian | Sp - Spanish |
| Jap. - Japanese | Turk. - Turkish |
| Lat. - Latin | Ven. - Venezualan |

We would like to thank the following for their help in providing the instruments that are pictured in this book. Academy Music, Church of the Covenant, Cleveland Institute of Music, Cleveland Orchestra, Halim El-Dabh (Professor of Ethnomusicology at Kent State University), Thomas Fries (Professor of Percussion at Hiram College), Robert Matson and Donald Miller (Percussionists with the Cleveland Orchestra), Terry Miller (Assistant Professor of Music History and Literature at Kent State University), Prospect Music, Emil Richards (Hollywood Studio Percussionist), Greg Selker, Mike Shellenbarger, Frank A. Stolarski and Dr. T. Temple Tuttle (Head of Ethnomusicology Studies, Music Department, Cleveland State University).

The authors would like to give special thanks to Donald Miller for the help he gave in the preparation of this work. The time spent in reading this text, his comments and suggestions are greatly appreciated.

Also thanks to Brenda Cunningham and Kirsten Faden for the long hours spent on typing and proofreading the manuscript.

# CONTENTS

Photographs by Joseph Adato and George Judy

# I.
# Alphabetical Listing
## of the
# Percussion Instruments

# A

**aeolian bells**

Suspended brass bars

**African goblet drum**

A two headed drum with an hour glass shape that is held under one arm. Pitch is changed when the ropes that connect the two heads are squeezed. Also known as a *talking drum*. See picture #1.

**African shakers**

Small enclosed wooden baskets, filled with seeds, and provided with a handle.

**African slit drums**

Drums made from the trunks of trees which are hollowed out with length-wise cuts to produce two tongues of different pitch and a resonating chamber. Two different tones can be produced by playing at the edge or rim. Played with hard wood sticks or small clubs. Also known as a *slit drum*. See picture #83.

**African tree drums**

A hollowed out log or wooden rectangular box in which one or more tongues have been cut into the lid. Each tongue will produce a different pitch. This instrument is used to imitate the sounds of African slit drums. Also known as a *jungle wood drum, log drum, tuned log* or *wooden gong*. See. picture #81.

**Afro-Brazilian drum**

A primitive drum which is made out of a hollowed out tree trunk covered with animal hide. It has a high sounding timbre.

**Afro-Brazilian metal bell**

A conical shaped metal bell on a handle that is struck with a metal beater.

**Afro-Brazilian musical bow**

An arched bow whose cord is rubbed with a piece of wood or animal bone.

**afuche**

There are two types of afuches, one of which is known as a cabasa. The authentic afuche is a dried hollow gourd with a net of beads loosely attached around the outside surface. See picture #2. The contemporary instrument, or cabasa, is a set of metal beads loosely wrapped around a serrated metal cylinder. See picture #21. Both instruments are played by turning the instrument with one hand while resting the beads in the palm of the other hand.

**agogo bells**

Two conical shaped cowbells, one larger than the other, each connected to opposite ends of a U shaped rod which is used as a handle. The cowbells are of different pitches and can be played with any hard mallet. See picture #3.

**air-raid siren**

An instrument which is hand cranked or electric. The sound is produced when a perforated rotating disk interrupts the flow of air creating an ascending and descending glissando effect. The instrument may be equipped with an additional crank that enables the performer to stop the sound immediatly. Also known as a *police siren, siren* or *warning siren*.

**alarm bell**

A cast bronze or brass bell equipped with a metal clapper. The clapper is pulled against the inside of the bell by a leather strap or rope which is attached to the end of the clapper. This bell can be of any size. Also known as a *ship's bell* or *storm bell*. See picture #4.

**Alpine herd cowbells**

*Tuned cowbells.* See picture #5.

**American Indian tom tom**

A two headed, roped tensioned drum, the heads of which are strung over a hollowed out tree trunk.

### ancient cymbals

Small pitched cymbals normally played in pairs by striking each together at the edge. They can also be suspended or mounted on a frame and struck with a metal, brass or plastic beater. Also known as *antique cymbals* or *Greek cymbals*. See picture #8.

### Andean jingle rattle

A rattle made out of dried fruit shells.

### angklung

Tuned bamboo tubes on a bamboo frame. Played by holding one end of the frame while shaking the tubes back and forth. Also known as a *bamboo rattle*. See picture #6.

### animal bells

Any type of bell hung around the neck of an animal. Can be made out of metal or wood.

### ankle beads

A bunched set of bean pods that are strung around the ankle.

### ankle bells

Any type of bells strung around the ankle. See picture #7.

### antique cymbals

Small pitched cymbals normally played in pairs by striking each together at the edge. They can also be suspended or mounted on a frame and struck with a metal, brass or plastic beater. Also known as *ancient cymbals* or *Greek cymbals*. See picture #8.

### anvil

Traditionally a large solid block of metal used by blacksmiths. Today, it can be any type of metal object that simulates the authentic anvil sound, i.e. iron pipes played with a hammer. See picture #93.

### Arabian hand drum

A goblet shaped hand held drum made out of clay or metal with sheepskin heads that are tightened by strings or tension rods. The drum is played with the fingers or open palm in both the center and edge of the head. Also known as a *derabucca, tarbourka, doumbek, dumbek* or *dumbeg*. See pictures #9 & #45.

### Arabian tablas

A bowl shaped leather tensioned drum of indefinite pitch.

### arched tree chimes

A series of suspended brass tubes of various lengths creating the shape of an arch.

### auto horn

Any mechanism that can duplicate the sound of an automobile horn. Also known as a *car horn, motor horn, taxi horn* or *bulb horn*. See picture #94.

# B

### Babylonian drum

A large tuned drum which is used in the composition 'Fiery Furnace' by Benjamin Britten. In it, the drum is tuned to D below bass clef.

### babys cry

A type of whistle that produces the sound of a babys cry.

### babys rattle

There are two types of baby rattles. One type produced a maraca sound and the other produces a multiple bell-like sound when shaken.

**balafon(e)**

A West African xylophone with gourd resonators that produce a buzz sound when played. See picture #10.

**bamboo rattle**

Tuned bamboo tubes on a bamboo frame. Played by holding one end of the frame while shaking the tubes back and forth. Also known as *angklungs*. See picture #6.

**bamboo scraper**

A hollow piece of bamboo with a series of vertical notches cut across the belly and opened at one end. Held in one hand and scraped with a thin piece of bamboo or metal rod.

**bamboo shaker**

A bamboo tube closed at both ends and filled with seed, shot, pebbles, etc. Held in the hand and shaken.

**bamboo slit logs**

A hollowed out bamboo log with a horizontal opening and an attached handle at one end. Sound can be produced either by striking the handle or striking the horizontal opening at the center. See picture #11.

**bamboo wind chimes**

Suspended pieces of bamboo which strike against each other when shaken. Also known as *wooden wind chimes* or *Japanese wood chimes*. See picture #95.

**barrel drum**

A large two headed drum which is placed horizontally. Each head produces two tones when played with the fingers or hand. See picture #12.

**Basler drum**

A rope tensioned, metal shell parade drum with wooden hoops.

**bass chimes**

Eight chimes that range from E below middle C to B just below middle C. Also known as *Parsifal chimes*.

**bass drum**

A large two headed drum which is normally 20″-36″ in diameter.

**bass drum with cymbal attached**

This refers to the situation in which one player has to play both concert bass drum and crash cymbals at the same time. One cymbal is mounted upside down to the shell of a concert bass drum and struck with another cymbal that is held in the player's hand. Simultaneously, the performer will strike the bass drum with a mallet held in the other hand.

**bass drum pedal with cymbal**

A small cymbal is attached to the rim of the bass drum facing the playing head. Attached to the bass drum pedal is a double beater which strikes both the bass drum and cymbal simultaneously. The cymbal beater is made out of metal and can be disengaged when not needed.

**bass xylophone**

A two octave xylophone whose range starts with G 1½ octaves below middle C and extending to G above middle C.

**bata drum**

An hour glass shaped drum with two heads, one larger than the other, which is played in a horizontal position with the fingers or hand. See picture #13.

**bell bar**

Part or all of a set of orchestra bells.

## bell chimes

Metal bars that usually come in sets of three or six, i.e. $B^b E^b G B^b E^b G$ that are placed over brass resonators producing a three note melody. Played with a soft covered mallet. Also known as *dinner chimes*.

## belled wooden spoons

A pair of wooden spoons with small bells attached to the handle.

## bell lyre

An aluminum keyboard percussion instrument in the shape of a lyre held in an upright position. Traditionally seen in marching bands. See picture #96.

## bell plate

A flat suspended piece of metal which is struck with a metal hammer. Can be of definite or indefinite pitch. Also known as *plate bells*. See picture #97.

## bell tree

A series of cup shaped bells mounted on a single rod in graduating sizes. Played with a brass mallet in a glissando fashion. Also known as *Pakistan tree bells*. See picture #14.

## bell wheel

A set of small bells that are attached to a revolving wheel.

## bendir

A one headed frame drum with snares inside the drum resting against the underside of the batter head.

## bin zasara

A series of small boards strung together with handles at each end. Played with a whip like motion to simulate the sound of a row of falling dominos. Also known as a *strung clapper*. See picture #15.

## bird whistle

Any type of whistle that produces the sounds of birds, i.e. Jay call, Canary, etc.

## board clappers

Two rectangular pieces of wood struck together. Both pieces are connected by a hinge at one end. The length and width can be of any size. Also known as a *slap stick, whip* or *wooden clapper*. See picture #82.

## boat whistle

There are several types, each producing a different type of boat whistle, i.e. steamboat, battleship, etc. See picture #98.

## bones

Two pairs of rectangular curved pieces of wood or hard plastic. The performer will hold one pair in each hand. One piece is held between the thumb and forefinger, the other between the forefinger and middle finger. A flick of the wrist will cause them to click together.

## bongos

Two small single headed drums of different diameters. Both are non-pitched, but tensioned approximately a 4th apart. Also known as *Cuban tom toms*. See picture #99.

## boobams

Two chromatic octaves of small single headed drums, the heads of which are made out of skin or plastic and mounted over long wooden resonators. See picture #16.

## bosuns pipe

A whistle used on board a ship before an announcement. See picture #100.

## brake drum

The brake wheel of an automobile. When struck, it produces a bell-like sound. See picture #17.

## brass wind chimes

Small suspended tubes of brass that strike against each other when shaken.

### Brazilian wooden blocks

Two wooden blocks, one which is grooved and the other smooth. The smooth block is rubbed across the grooves of the other causing a rasping sound. Very similar to a guiro.

### bronze sheets

Thin pieces of bronze sheets that when shaken produce the sound of a high-pitch thunder crack. This instrument can also be suspended and struck with a wooden mallet or steel hammer.

### Buddha temple bell

A cup shaped bell which rests on a cushion and is played on the inner rim with a leather, rubber or cloth covered mallet. Also known as a *Japanese temple bell, prayer bell, temple cup bell, dobaci, temple cup gong, cup gong, temple bell, cup bell* or *dabachi*. See picture #18.

### bulb horn

An automobile horn which is played by squeezing the bulb. Also known as a *taxi horn*. See picture #94.

### bull roarer

A thin piece of wood attached to a string which is whirled in the air producing a howling sound. The faster the instrument is whirled the higher the pitch. Also known as a *thunder stick* or *whizzer*. See picture #19.

### bumbass

A pole with two small cymbals on top and small sleigh bells immediately below. Attached to the pole farther down is a small drum. A thin wire is strung from the top of the pole, across the drum head, and attached to the bottom of the pole. A small beater, which is fastened to the wire, hits the drum when the wire is plucked. The cymbals and jingles are played when the pole is struck against the ground. Also known as a *devil's violin*.

### burma bell

A pagoda shaped bell which, when struck, gives a long sustaining sound. A vibrato can be created by striking the bell at either end causing the bell to twirl. Also known as a *Burmese temple bell* or *Kyeezee bell*. See picture #20.

### Burmese temple bell. *See burma bell.*

### button gong

A round, heavy bronze plate of definite pitch with a raised boss or nipple in the center. The instrument is struck on the raised boss or nipple with a felt or cloth covered mallet. Different sizes will produce different pitches. Also known as a *domed gong, gong, nipple gong,* or *java gong*. See picture #47.

### buzz marimba

A keyboard mallet instrument with skin membranes in the resonators which cause a buzzing sound when played. Also known as *nabimba*.

# C

### cabasa

There are two types of cabasas, one of which is known as an afuche. The cabasa is a set of metal beads that are loosely wrapped around a serrated metal cylinder. Also known as a *cockolo* or *metal cabasa*. See picture #21. The authentic afuche is a dried hollow gourd with a net of beads loosely attached around the outside surface. See picture #2. Both instruments are played by turning the instrument with one hand while resting the beads in the palm of the other hand.

### camel bells

A graduated series of cylindrical or conical shaped metal bells. They are attached to a rope, one inside each other, or suspended individually in a row and shaken. Also known as *Persian temple bells*. See picture #22.

### cannon shot

A sound effect created by A) a cannon B) striking a large bass drum as hard as possible in the center of the drum or C) shooting off a rifle in an extremely large oil barrel.

### car horn

Any mechanism that can duplicate the sound of an automobile horn. Also known as an *auto horn, bulb horn, motor horn* or *taxi horn*. See picture #94.

### carillon

A large, bronze bell with a clapper inside that is normally found in church towers. If not available, chimes may be substituted. Also known as *cast bells, church bells* or *steeple bells*. See picture #23.

### castanets

A pair of hollow, circular wooden clappers that are traditionally made from ebony or granadilla, but can also be made from plastic or any other hard wood. This instrument was originally held in the hand, i.e. Spanish Flamenco dancers, but is also found mounted on a paddle or a board.

### cast bells

Large, bronze bells with clappers that are found in church towers. If not available, chimes may be substituted. Also known as *carillons, church bells* or *steeple bells*. See picture #23.

### caxixi

A Brazilian rattle made from a woven wickerwork basket with a gourd bottom that is filled with dried seeds. Different sounds can be produced when the seeds strike the basket or gourd surface. See picture #24.

### chareston cymbal

A very early form of the hi-hat. It consists of two wooden plates with small cymbals attached to the inside facing each other. A spring is used to keep the cymbals apart and by stepping down on the top foot plate, the cymbals would make contact.

### charleston

Two cymbals mounted on a metal rod operated by a foot mechanism which brings the two cymbals together. Also known as a *foot cymbal, high hat, hi-hat, pedal cymbal* or *sock cymbal*.

### cheese box

A very low pitched wood block struck with a soft yarn mallet. This term originated from the wooden boxes used in carrying Philadelphia brand cream cheese.

### cheese grater

A kitchen aid used to grate cheese. Any type of metal scraper can be substituted.

### chimes

Normally a 1½ octave set of metal tubes suspended vertically on a frame and played with a rawhide mallet. Extended ranges are available. Also known as *tubular bells* or *tubular chimes*.

### Chimta India row jingles

Two sticks attached at one end with small jingles mounted to the outside of each stick. Played by opening and closing the thongs or by shaking the stick. See picture #25.

### Chinese Confucian bells

A 2¼ octave set of micro-tonal temple bells that are played with soft beaters to produce approximately 28 tones per octave. These bells can be arranged in groups of 3, 5, 7 or 9 and struck individually or glissed in a horizontal or vertical fashion. Also known as *Chinese tree bells* or *dharma bells*. See picture #26.

### Chinese cup gongs

A series of graduating, suspended, cup shaped bowls of different pitches. See picture #27.

### Chinese cymbal

A cymbal with upturned edges and a raised, square center. See picture #28.

### Chinese drum

A small two headed drum with pig skin heads tacked or nailed onto a wooden shell with or without dragons and other Chinese designs painted on the heads. See picture #29.

### Chinese hand drum

A two headed drum with a handle. Attached to the shell on each side is a knotted cord. The drum is played with quick turns of the wrist causing the cords to strike the heads. Also known as a *Chinese paper drum, rattle drum* or *snake dance drum*. See picture #30.

### Chinese paper drum. *See* Chinese hand drum.

### Chinese temple blocks

A series of five rounded or squared blocks of wood that are hollowed out and struck with a soft mallet. Traditionally tuned to a pentatonic scale. Also known as *dragon's mouths, fish drums, Korean blocks, temple blocks* or *wooden fish*. See picture #31.

### Chinese tom tom

A large two headed barrel shaped drum. The shell is made out of wood and the heads, which are tacked onto the barrel, are pig skin. Iron rings are mounted on the shell of the drum which produces a rattle when the drum is struck. See picture #32.

### Chinese tree bells

A 2¼ octave set of micro-tonal temple bells that are played with soft beaters to produce approximately 28 tones per octave. These bells can be arranged in groups of 3, 5, 7 or 9 and struck individually or glissed in a horizontal or vertical fashion. Also known as *Chinese Confucian bells* or *dharma bells*. See picture #26.

### Chinese wood block

A rectangular block of wood with a horizontal slit near both playing surfaces which serves as a sound chamber. Played with a wooden stick or hard rubber mallet.

### Chinese wooden drum

A drum made out of camphor wood and shaped like a disk with a circular cut in the bottom that acts as a resonator. A very short raised disk, where the drum is struck, is located on top. The drum stands on three short wooden legs that are attached to the bottom. The mallets that are used can be xylophone mallets or mallets made of hardwood. The sound is similar to a temple block. Also known as a *mokubio, mokugyo, Japanese wood block* or *Japanese wooden drum*.

### ching

1) A pair of small cup shaped finger cymbals of Thailand which are thick and about 2¼″ in diameter. See picture #33. 2) A Korean bending gong which descends in pitch when struck with a soft beater.

### ching-a-ring

A metal tambourine which attaches to the metal rod of the hi-hat. See picture #34.

### chocallo

A cylindrical metal tube filled with beads, pebbles, shot or seeds that is played by shaking the tube back and forth. Also known as a *metal shaker, metal tube, metal tube shaker* or *tubo*. See picture #35.

### church bell

Large, bronze bells with clappers that are found in church towers. If not available, chimes may be substituted. Also known as *carillon, cast bells* or *steeple bells*. See picture #23.

### clash (crash) cymbals

A pair of cymbals that are struck together to produce a "crash" sound.

### claves

A pair of cylindrical pieces of hard wood which are struck together to produce rhythmic beats. Sometimes one of the sticks will have a cut-away design to act as a sound chamber. Also known as *Cuban sticks*. See picture #36.

### clay rattle

A maraca with a clay head

### clog box

A rectangular block of wood with a horizontal slit near both playing surfaces which serves as a sound chamber. Played with a wooden stick or hard rubber mallet. Also known as a *tap box* or *wood block*.

**cockolo**

The contemporary version of an afuche which consists of a set of metal beads loosely wrapped around a serrated metal cylinder. It is played by turning the instrument with one hand while resting the beads in the palm of the other hand. Also known as a *cabasa* or *metal cabasa*. See picture #21.

**cocktail drum**

A floor tom tom with a bass drum pedal attached to the bottom head and a suspended cymbal attached to the top shell. Usually played with brushes.

**coconut shells**

A hollowed out coconut or wood shell that is cut in half. Both halves are used to produce the sound of walking or galloping horses by striking the open ends against a hard surface. Also known as *hoofbeats* or *horses hooves*. See picture #37.

**cog rattle**

Most commonly known as a ratchet which is an instrument that reproduces the sound effect of a stick running along a picket fence. See picture #38.

**coilspring**

An automobile coil spring that is suspended and struck with a metal beater. Also known as *wire coils*. See picture #102.

**Colgrass drum**

A predecessor of the roto tom that was invented by percussionist/composer Michael Colgrass. These drums consisted of cardboard shells and small wing nuts used for tuning.

**Colombian jungle drum**

A hollowed out tree trunk with a hole in the middle that is capable of producing different sounds when struck with a wooden beater.

**concert tom toms**

A series of two or more single headed drums in different sizes.

**concussion blocks**

Two hard rectangular blocks of wood with slightly curved sides that are clapped together to produce sharp penetrating accents in Japanese and Chinese music. See picture #39.

**concussion sticks**

A pair of short wooden sticks which can either be struck on the ground or struck together.

**conga drum**

A single headed, elongated barrel or conical shell drum which is normally played with the hands. The drum is equipped with tension rods and comes in three sizes: small (quinto), medium (conga) and large (tumbadora). The diameter of a conga is usually 11¾". See picture #103.

**conical drum**

Any drum in which each end is a considerable difference in diameter from each other, i.e. Arabian hand drum. See picture #9.

**contra bass marimba**

A marimba which extends a perfect 4th lower than most bass marimbas and is played with large wool wound mallets.

**cowbell**

A clapperless elongated conical shaped metal bell which is normally played with a wooden stick.

**crash cymbal(s)**

When indicated in a symphonic setting, it refers to a pair of cymbals struck together. (Also known as *manual cymbals* or *hand cymbals*.) When used with a drum set, it refers to a suspended cymbal(s).

### cricket clickers

An instrument which simulated the sound effect of crickets. The instrument is held between the thumb and finger and played by depressing and releasing the clicker. See picture #40.

### crow call

A whistle which imitates the sound of a crow. See picture #104.

### crystals

Suspended pieces of glass which strike each other when shaken. Also known as *glass wind chimes.*

### Cuban sticks

A pair of cylindrical pieces of hard wood which are struck together to produce rhythmic beats. Sometimes one of the sticks will have a cut-away design to act as a sound chamber. Also known as *claves.* See picture #36.

### Cuban tom toms

Two small single headed drums of different diameters. Both are non-pitched, but tensioned approximately a 4th apart. Also known as *bongos.* See picture #99.

### cuckoo call

A two tone whistle which produces the sound of a cuckoo bird. The instrument is played by pressing and releasing the finger on top of the fingerhole while blowing into the instrument. See picture #105.

### cuica

A one headed tensioned drum. Inside, a thin wooden stick is attached through the head. The drum is played by rubbing the stick with a damp cloth or wetted hand to produce a friction which vibrates the head. See picture #41.

### cup bells

A cup shaped bell which rests on a cushion and is played on the inner rim with a leather, rubber or cloth covered mallet. Also known as *Buddha temple bells, Japanese temple bells, prayer bells, temple cup bells, dobaci, temple cup gongs, cup gongs, temple bells* or *dabachi.* See picture #18.

### cup glasses

A set of drinking glasses tuned by filling with water to different levels and struck with a light wooden beater or rubbed with a moistened finger. The glasses can be arranged to produce an entire scale. The glasses should sit on a cloth. Also known as a *glass harp, musical glasses* or *tuned glasses.*

### cup gong

A cup shaped bell which rests on a cushion and is played on the inner rim with a leather, rubber or cloth covered mallet. Also known as a *Buddha temple bell, Japanese temple bell, prayer bell, temple cup bell, dobaci, temple cup gong, temple bell, cup bell* or *dabachi.* See picture #18.

### cyclone whistle

A cylindrical metal whistle which, when blown into, causes a disk inside to rotate and produce a howling glissando effect. Also known as a *mouth siren* or *siren whistle.* See picture #42.

### cylindrical drum

A two headed snare drum which can be tensioned by rope or screws. In the 16th C., the drum was normally 20″-28″ in depth and 20″-22″ in diameter, although some were larger. By the 18th C., the depth and width were the same. The wooden shell was replaced by a metal shell. Today, a military snare drum can be substituted.

### cylindrical wood block

A two-toned tubular wood block made out of hardwood. Both blocks are partially hollowed out with slits at both openings. Played with a wooden stick. Also known as a *tubular wood block* or *wooden agogos.* See picture #43.

### cymbals

Circular metal plates which can be played in pairs or individually.

**cymbal tongs**

   Two small cymbals each attached to the end of a springlike tong with the inner plates of the cymbals facing each other. When the tongs are pressed together, the cymbals clash against each other. Also known as *metal castanets*. See picture #44.

**cymbal tree**

   A graduating series of suspended cymbals, placed one on top of each other, on a stand. Normally played with a metal beater in a glissando fashion. Also known as *tree cymbals*.

# D

**dabachi**

   A cup shaped bell which rests on a cushion and is played on the inner rim with a leather, rubber or cloth covered mallet. Also known as *Buddha temple bell, Japanese temple bell, prayer bell, temple cup bell, dobaci, temple cup gong, cup gong, temple bell* or *cup bell*. See picture #18.

**da-daiko**

   A large two headed barrel shaped drum about 5 ft. long and 6 ft. in diameter. The drum is hung on a stand and played with two heavy lacquered beaters in a left to right sequence. The smaller version is called a *ko-daiko*.

**dagga**

   A low sounding tabla drum made out of metal. The head is made in three sections. A black patch is pasted to the head a little off center. There is a second skin approximately 1″ in width which runs around the outer circumference of the drumhead. The drum is played with the fingers and hand striking the various surfaces of the drum. Also known as a *duggi*. See picture #84.

**dai-shoko**

   A large suspended bronze gong of Japan that is played with two knobbed beaters.

**derabucca**

   A goblet shaped hand held drum made out of clay or metal with sheepskin heads that are tightened by strings or tension rods. The drum is played with the fingers or open palm in both the center and edge of the head. Also known as a *Arabian hand drum, doumbek, dumbeg, dumbek* or *tarbourka*. See picture #9 & #45.

**devil's violin**

   A pole with two small cymbals on top and small sleigh bells immediately below. Attached to the pole farther down is a small drum. A thin wire is strung from the top of the pole, across the drum head, and attached to the bottom of the pole. A small beater, which is fastened to the wire, hits the drum when the wire is plucked. The cymbals and jingles are played when the pole is struck against the ground. Also known as a *bumbass*.

**dharma bells**

   A 2¼ octave set of micro-tonal temple bells that are played with soft beaters to produce approximately 28 tones per octave. These bells can be arranged in groups of 3, 5, 7 or 9 and struck individually or glissed in a horizontal or vertical fashion. Also known as *Chinese Confucian bells* or *Chinese tree bells*. See picture #26.

**dholak**

   A small Indian drum made from a hollowed out block of wood with two heads of the same diameter. The heads are tensioned by lacing that passes through small metal rings. Also known as a *dholki* or *dolak*. See picture #46.

**dholki.** *See dholak.*

**dinner bell**

   A small steel bell with a clapper inside and a handle; used to signal dinner time.

**dinner chimes**

   Metal bars that usually come in sets of three or six, i.e. B♭ E♭ G B♭ E♭ G, that are placed over brass resonators producing a three note melody. Played with a soft covered mallet. Also known as *bell chimes*.

### dobaci

A cup shaped bell which rests on a cushion and is played on the inner rim with a leather, rubber or cloth covered mallet. Also known as a *Japanese temple bell, prayer bell, temple cup bell, temple cup gong, temple bell, cup bell, dabachi* or *Buddha temple bell*. See picture #18.

### dog's bark

A small drum made out of a cylindrical piece of wood or metal, one end of which is covered with a skin. In the center of the skin is a small hole through which a gut string protrudes. A moistened or rosined piece of leather or canvas is pulled along the string away from the drum producing the sound of a dog's bark. The larger version is known as a *lion's roar*. Also known as a *jackdaw* or *string drum*. See picture #108.

### doira

An eastern European hand drum similar to a large tambourine without jingles.

### dolak

A small Indian drum made from a hollowed out block of wood with two heads of the same diameter. The heads are tensioned by lacing that passes through small metal rings. Also known as a *dholak* or *dholki*. See picture #46.

### domed gong

A round, heavy bronze plate of definite pitch with a raised boss or nipple in the center. The instrument is struck on the raised boss or nipple with a felt or cloth covered mallet. Different sizes will produce different pitches. Also known as a *button gong, gong, Java gong* or *nipple gong*. See picture #47.

### double conical drum

A drum in which the center has the largest diameter and tapers toward both ends.

### doumbek

A goblet shaped hand held drum made out of clay or metal with sheepskin heads that are tightened by strings or tension rods. The drum is played with the fingers or open palm in both the center and edge of the head. Also known as an *Arabian hand drum, derabucca, dumbeg, dumbek* or *tarbourka*. See pictures #9 & #45.

### dragon's mouths

A series of five rounded or squared blocks of wood that are hollowed out and struck with a soft mallet. Traditionally tuned to a pentatonic scale. Also known as *Chinese temple blocks, fish drums, Korean blocks, temple blocks* or *wooden fish*. See picture #31.

### drum gong

A circular heavy metal plate made out of bronze with deep curved rims and a flat ornamented surface. It is suspended and played with beaters made out of felt or cloth. Also known as a *kettle gong, metal drum* or *tam tam*. See picture #85.

### drum set

A standard set of drums which includes a snare drum, tom toms (both mounted and floor tom tom), a pedaled bass drum, hi-hat, and any number of suspended cymbals. Played by one person. Also known as a *trap set*.

### duck call

A whistle which imitates the sound of a duck. See picture #106.

### duggi

A low sounding tabla drum made out of metal. The head is made in three sections. A black patch is pasted to the head a little off center. There is a second skin approximately 1″ in width which runs around the outer circumference of the drumhead. The drum is played with the fingers and hand striking various surfaces of the drum. Also known as a *dagga*. See picture #84.

### dumbeg

A goblet shaped hand held drum made out of clay or metal with sheepskin heads that are tightened by strings or tension rods. The drum is played with the fingers or open palm in both the center and edge of the head. Also known as an *Arabian hand drum, derabucca, doumbek, dumbek* or *tarbourka*. See pictures #9 & #45.

### dumbek. *See dumbeg.*

# E

**elephant bells**

Spherical shaped bells made out of brass alloy. The open bottom consists of claw-like pointed prongs and inside a clapper is attached. The diameter ranged from ¾″-4″. Also known as *sarna bells*.

# F

**field drum**

A snare drum which normally ranges between 9″-12″ in depth and 15″ in diameter with gut or metal snares. The drum should produce a crisp and dry timbre. Also known as a *military drum*.

**fighter's bell**

A bowl shaped bell made out of brass that is played with a hammer on the side of the bell. Also known as a *fire bell* or *trip gong*. See picture #48.

**finger bell**

A small bell which produces a single tone used in hotel lobbies to call for service. Also known as a *service bell* or *tap bell*. See picture #49.

**finger cymbal(s)**

Small cymbals about 2″ in diameter that can either be held between the thumb and forefinger, one in each hand, or mounted on tongs or spring board. Normally played in pairs by striking the edges together or by striking the underside of each cymbal together. When mounted, they are also known as *cymbal tongs, metal castanets* or *mounted metal castanets*. See picture #107.

**fire bell**

A bowl shaped bell made out of brass that is played with a hammer on the side of the bell. Also known as a *fighter's bell* or *trip gong*. See picture #48.

**fish drums**

A series of five rounded or squared blocks of wood that are hollowed out and struck with a soft mallet. Traditionally tuned to a pentatonic scale. Also known as *Chinese temple blocks, dragon's mouth, Korean blocks, temple blocks* or *wooden fish*. See picture #31.

**flexatone**

A sheet of spring steel attached at one end of a metal frame. On both sides of the steel are attached two hard beaters. The sound is produced when the player shakes the metal frame while bending the steel with the thumb. This causes the beaters to strike the sheet while the pitch is changing. See picture #50.

**fog horn**

A whistle which is made out of three wooden or metal pipes each having a different pitch. They are attached to each other, but are blown through one mouthpiece. The sound is usually low pitched. Also known as a *ship's whistle* or *steamboat whistle*. See picture #118.

**foil rattle**

A large, thin, suspended sheet of metal that produces the sound of thunder when shook. Also known as a *thunder sheet*.

**foot bell**

A bell used as a car horn in India. It produces two pitches by pressing and depressing a button on top of the bell. See picture #51.

**foot cymbal**

Two cymbals mounted on a metal rod operated by a foot pedal mechanism which brings the two cymbals together. Also known as a *charleston, high-hat, hi-hat, pedal cymbal* or *sock cymbal*.

**four-row xylophone**

The predecessor to today's xylophone the bars of which were laid out on straw ropes with the accidentals on the outer rows. Some of the accidentals were duplicated to help facilitate certain passages. Played with spoon shaped beaters made out of hardwood or horn. The instrument is extremely difficult to obtain, so the parts are normally played on the xylophone.

## frame drum

A headed tambourine without jingles. Played with a hard or soft beater, with the fingertips, or ball of the hand. Also known as a *hand drum*. See picture #52.

## frame rattle

Rattling objects that are attached to some type of a frame which they strike, i.e. tambourine.

## friction drum

There are two types of friction drums. One type is known as a cuica which is a one headed tensioned drum. Inside, a thin wooden stick is attached through the head. The drum is played by rubbing the stick with a damp cloth or wetted hand to produce a friction which vibrates the head. See picture #41. The second type is known as a lion's roar which is made out of a cylindrical piece of wood or metal, one opening of which is covered with a skin. In the center of the skin is a small hole through which a gut string protrudes. A moistened or rosined piece of leather or canvas is pulled along the string away from the drum producing the sound of a lion's roar. The smaller version is known as a dog's bark. Also known as a *jackdaw* or *string drum*. See picture #108.

## frog call

A whistle that imitates the sound of a frog.

## frying pans

Different size standard kitchen frying pans mounted upside down on a wooden board. Produces a gong-like effect when played in the center with a rubber mallet.

# G

## gamelan gong

Nipple gongs that have a definite pitch but do not sustain. These gongs are used more for their rhythmic pulse rather than producing an authentic scale. Played on the raised boss. See picture #53.

## geophone

An object similar to a rain machine or wind machine. The difference being that calf heads are used as the shell. Pellets or any small objects are placed inside and as the drum revolves, a very real ocean effect is created.

## ghungroo tambourine

A tambourine with sleigh bells attached instead of the traditional jingles.

## glass harmonica

A series of glass bowls that are tuned depending on their size and mounted in a vertical position on a rotating spindle. To produce a sound, the performer places a dampened finger tip against the rim of the glass while it rotates.

## glass harp

A set of drinking glasses tuned by filling with water to different levels and struck with a light wooden beater or rubbed with a moistened finger. The glasses can be arranged to produce an entire scale. The glasses should sit on a cloth. Also known as *cup glasses, musical glasses* or *tuned glasses*.

## glass wind chimes

Suspended pieces of glass which strike each other when shaken. Also known as *crystals*.

## goblet drum

A ceramic, goblet shaped drum the head of which is attached to the base by means of small ropes laced to the head and tied to a metal hoop. See picture #54.

## gong

A round, heavy bronze plate of definite pitch with a raised boss or nipple in the center. The instrument is struck on the raised boss or nipple with a felt or cloth covered mallet. Different sizes will produce different pitches. Also known as a *button gong, domed gong* or *nipple gong*. See picture #47.

## gong bass drum

A one headed bass drum.

### gourd

A scraped instrument used in Latin American music. It is a hollowed out calabash with notches cut into the upper body and scraped with a stick. Also known as a *gourd scraper, guiro, rasp, rasper, rasping stick, scraper, scratcher, wooden scraper* or *wooden scratcher*. See picture #56.

### gourd drum

A hollowed out calabash shell the base of which has been cut off and replaced with a skin head.

### gourd rattle

A hollowed out calabash filled with pebbles or seeds and shaken by means of a hemp holder. Also known as a *vessel rattle*. See picture #55.

### gourd scraper

A scraped instrument used in Latin American music. It is a hollowed out calabash with notches cut into the upper body and scraped with a stick. Also known as a *gourd, guiro, rasp, rasper, rasping stick, scraper, scratcher, wooden scraper* or *wooden scratcher*. See picture #56.

### gourd water drum

A hollowed out gourd which is filled with water and played with sticks.

### Greek cymbals

Small pitched cymbals normally played in pairs by striking each other at the edge. They can also be suspended or mounted on a frame and struck with a metal, brass or plastic beater. Also known as *ancient cymbals* or *antique cymbals*. See picture #8.

### guiro

A scraped instrument used in Latin American music. It is a hollowed out calabash with notches cut into the upper body and scraped with a stick. Also known as a *gourd, gourd scraper, rasp, rasper, rasping stick, scraper, scratcher, wooden scraper* or *wooden scratcher*. See picture #56.

# H

### hammer

A hardware store hammer used to pound nails, a large wooden type as used in circuses, or a sledge hammer such as in Mahler's 6th Symphony.

### hand bells

Chromatically tuned brass bells which are equipped with a handle and clapper.

### hand cymbals

When indicated in a symphonic setting, it refers to a pair of cymbals struck together. Also known as crash cymbals or manual cymbals.

### hand drum

A headed tambourine without jingles. Played with the hand or soft beaters, with the fingertips, or ball of the hand. Also known as a *frame drum*. See picture #52.

### harness bells

A set of non-pitched small bells which are attached to a handle or strap and shaken. Also known as *sleigh bells*. See picture #115.

### hat

A stick with a metal top in the shape of a crescent with other ornaments and symbols from which small bells and jingles are suspended. The instrument is played by shaking the stick or pounding on the floor. Also known as a *jingling Johnnie, pavillon* or *Turkish crescent*.

### herd cowbells

A non-pitched metal bell with a clapper inside that is hung around the neck of an animal.

### high-hat

Two cymbals mounted on a metal rod operated by a foot pedal mechanism which brings the two cymbals together. Also known as a *charleston, foot cymbal, hi-hat, pedal cymbal* or *sock cymbal*.

**hi-hat.** *See* **high-hat.**

**hoof beats**

A hollowed out coconut or wood shell which is cut in half. Both halves are used to produce the sound of walking or galloping horses by striking the open ends against a hard surface. Also known as *coconut shells* or *horses hooves*. See picture #37.

**horses hooves.** *See* **hoof beats.**

**hour-glass drum**

A two headed drum the shell of which is in the shape of an hour glass. Rope is used to attach both heads to the shell. The drum is held under the arm and tension is applied by squeezing the arm against the body, thus changing the pitch. See picture #57.

# I

**Indian bell strap**

Small bells made out of hardened sheet brass attached to a leather strap and placed around the ankle. Each bell is normally ⅝" in diameter with crosswise slits. Each strap contains 16-32 bells depending upon its width. Also known as *ankle bells*. See picture #7.

**Indian chimes**

Very small bells, i.e. sarna or ankle bells.

**Indian drum**

A single or double headed drum the shell of which is made out of wood or burnt clay. The heads are tightened with cords and played with club-like mallets that produce rattling sounds. Noisier sounds can be produced by using beaters with hollow heads that are filled with pebbles or seeds.

**Indian jingles**

A set of tambourine jingles mounted on wooden frames and held one in each hand. They are played in pairs by striking the flat ends against each other. See picture #58.

**iron chains**

A linked chain with or without handles that is either struck against a steel plate or on the floor or shaken.

**iron pipe**

A cylindrical metal object that can be used to duplicate the sound of an anvil. See picture #93.

# J

**jackdaw**

A drum which is made out of a cylindrical piece of wood or metal one opening of which is covered with a skin. In the center of the skin is a small hole through which a gut string protrudes. A moistened or rosined piece of leather or canvas is pulled along the string away from the drum producing the sound of a lion's roar. The smaller version is known as a dog's bark. Also known as a *lion's roar* or *string drum*. See picture #108.

**Japanese metal bar(s)**

Four pitched metal bars suspended over resonators that are shaped like cowbells.

**Japanese temple bell**

A cup shaped bell which rests on a cushion and is played on the inner rim with a leather, rubber or cloth covered mallet. Also known as a *prayer bell, Buddha temple bell, temple cup bell, dobaci, temple cup gong, cup gong, temple bell, cup bell* or *dabachi*. See picture #18.

**Japanese tree bells**

Various sizes and shaped bells from Japan that are strung together in a bell tree fashion on a large frame. The bells are not necessarily strung in accordance with their pitch. They can be played individually or in a glissando fashion with a metal beater.

### Japanese wood block

A drum made out of camphor wood and shaped like a disk with a circular cut in the bottom that acts as a resonator. A very short raised disk which is where the drum is struck is located on top. The drum stands on three short wooden legs that are attached to the bottom. The mallets that can be used are xylophone mallets or any mallet made of hardwood. The sound is similar to a temple block. Also known as a *Chinese wooden drum, Japanese wooden drum, mokubio* or *mokugyo.*

### Japanese wood chimes

Suspended pieces of bamboo which strike against each other when shaken. Also known as *bamboo wind chimes* or *wooden wind chimes.* See picture #95.

### Japanese wooden drum

A drum made out of camphor wood and shaped like a disk with a circular cut in the bottom that acts as a resonator. A very short raised disk which is located on top is where the drum is struck. The drum stands on three short wooden logs that are attached to the bottom. The mallets that are used can be xylophone mallets or any mallet made of hardwood. The sound is similar to a temple block. Also known as a *Chinese wooden drum, Japanese wood block, mokubio* or *mokugyo.*

### Java gong

A round, heavy bronze plate of definite pitch with a raised boss or nipple in the center. The instrument is struck on the raised boss or nipple with a felt or cloth covered mallet. Different sizes will produce different pitches. Also known as a *button gong, domed gong, gong* or *nipple gong.* See picture #47.

### jawbone (of an ass)

The lower jawbone of a mule or donkey that is dried and played with the fist to allow the teeth to rattle. The contemporary version is known as a *vibraslap.* See picture #59.

### jaw (Jew's) harp

An iron frame with a flexible metal tongue. The harp is placed in the mouth between the teeth. The top of the metal tongue is plucked while using the mouth and teeth as a resonator. See picture #60.

### Jew's harp. *See* jaw (Jew's) harp.

### jingle

A small, circular, high sounding metal plate about 2″ in diameter with slightly bent rims. Found on tambourines, mounted in pairs.

### jingle stick

A stick with jingles attached that is struck against the ground.

### jingling Johnnie

A stick with a metal top in the shape of a crescent with other ornaments and symbols from which small bells and jingles are suspended. The instrument is played by shaking the stick or pounding it on the floor. Also known as a *hat, pavillon,* or *Turkish crescent.*

### jug

A large bottle with a small hole. Air is blown across the hole in the same manner as a flute.

### jungle wood drum

A hollowed out log or wooden rectangular box in which one or more tongues have been cut into the lid. Each tongue produces a different pitch. This instrument is used to imitate the sounds of African slit drums. Also known as an *African tree drum, log drum, tuned log* or *wooden gong.* See picture #81.

# K

### kalimba

A series of tuned metal tongues that are attached to a wooden box over a sound hole. The instrument is played by plucking the tongues. Also known as a *sanza* or *thumb piano.* See picture #61.

### kazoo

A small metal tube with a hole on the topside that is covered by a piece of membrane. Played by humming into the mouthpiece. See picture #109.

### kettle drum

A drum made out of copper or fiberglass bowls shaped like kettles that produce definite pitches. The drums are single headed and usually equipped with a foot pedal for tuning changes. The drums are played with felt mallets of different hardnesses. Also known as *timpany*.

### kettle gong

A circular, heavy metal plate made out of bronze with deep curved rims and a flat ornamented surface. It is suspended and played with beaters made out of felt or cloth. Also known as a *drum gong, metal drum* or *tam tam*. See picture #85.

### keyboard glockenspiel

A set of orchestra bells that are placed inside of a small upright piano. The instrument is normally played by a pianist. Also known as *keyboard orchestra bells* or *keyed glockenspiel.**

### keyboard orchestra bells *See* keyboard glockenspiel.

### keyboard xylophone

A set of 3½ to 4 octave xylophone bars placed inside a small upright piano. It is played in the same manner as a piano which the keys activate the hammers which strike against the wooden bars.

### key chimes

Suspended house or car keys that strike against each other when shaken. See picture #110.

### keyed glockenspiel

A set of orchestra bells that are placed inside a small upright piano. The instrument is normally played by a pianist. Also known as a *keyboard glockenspiel* or *keyboard orchestra bells.**

### khartals India hand jingles

Tambourine type jingles attached to a large frame with handles on each end. The instrument is held in a horizontal position with both hands and shaken. See picture #62.

### klaxon horn

An automobile horn from the 1930's that is hand cranked. See picture #63.

*\* Although glockenspiel is a German term, its usage in the English language is so common that it has become an acceptable English term.*

### ko-daiko

A small two headed barrel shaped drum about 26″ long and 22″ wide. The drum is hung or rests on a stand and is played with two heavy lacquered beaters in a left to right sequence. The larger version is called da-daiko.

### Korean blocks

A series of five rounded or squared blocks of wood that are hollowed out and struck with a soft mallet. Traditionally tuned to a pentatonic scale. Also known as *Chinese temple blocks, dragon's mouths, fish drum, temple blocks* or *wooden fish*. See picture #31.

### Korean multiboard whip

Six small hard wood bars that are normally 13⅝″ in length, 2³⁄₁₆″ wide at the bottom and 1¾″ on top. There are two holes at the top and all six boards are loosely held together by a cord which runs through the holes. The boards are separated by hand and pushed together to produce a short ratchet type effect.

### kyeezee bell

A pagoda shaped bell which when struck gives a long sustaining sound. A vibrato can be created by striking the bell at either end, causing the bell to twirl. Also known as a *burma bell* or *Burmese temple bell*. See picture #20.

# L

### lava rocks

Volcanic rocks that are held one or two in each hand and struck together.

### lion's roar

A drum which is made out of a cylindrical piece of wood or metal one opening of which is covered with a skin. In the center of the skin, is a small hole through which a gut string protrudes. A moistened or rosined piece of leather or canvas is pulled along the string away from the drum producing the sound of a lion's roar. The smaller version is known as a dog's bark. Also known as a *jackdaw* or *string drum*. See picture #108.

### lithophone

A keyboard instrument the bars of which are made out of stone disks and played with a hard hammer. Also known as *stone disks* or *stone chimes*.

### log drum

A hollowed out log or wooden rectangular box in which one or more tongues have been cut into the lid. Each tongue produces a different pitch. This instrument is used to imitate the sounds of African slit drums. Also known as *African tree drum, jungle wood drum, tuned log* or *wooden gong*. See picture #81.

### long drum

A wooden shell drum ranging from 20″-30″ in depth and 16″-20″ in diameter with calf skin heads placed on narrow wooden hoops. Four to six gut strings lie across the bottom head. The drum is equipped with three adjustable legs which enable the drum to stand off the ground. The timbre of the drum is that of a dark, muffled sound. Also known as a *Mercenary Soldiers drum*.

### loo-jon

A large wooden box which is partitioned into small sections that act as resonators. One end of the box is open exposing the different resonators. Over these resonators are attached metal plates of different pitches. The range depends on how many partitions are built into the box. The instrument is played with soft felt or yarn mallets. Also known as a *lujon* or *metal log drum*.

### lotus flute

A whistle made out of a long tube with a slide at one end. An ascending and descending glissando is produced by moving the slide back and forth while blowing into the mouthpiece. Also known as a *slide whistle, song whistle, swanee piccolo* or *swanee whistle*. See picture #116.

### low boy

Two cymbals on a metal rod operated by a foot pedal mechanism which brings the two cymbals together. The height of the instrument is about 13″. An early version of the hi-hat. See picture #111.

### lujons

A large wooden box which is partitioned into small sections that act as resonators. One end of the box is open exposing the different resonators. Over these resonators are attached metal plates of different pitches. The range depends on how many partitions are built into the box. The instrument is played with soft felt or yarn mallets. Also known as a *loo-jon* or *metal log drum*.

# M

### mandira

Finger cymbals of India. Also known as *manjira*. See picture #65.

### manjira. *See* mandira.

### manual cymbals

When indicated in a symphonic setting, it refers to a pair of cymbals struck together. Also known as *crash cymbals* or *hand cymbals*.

### maraca(s)

A rattle made out of gourd, clay or wood which is attached to a handle and filled with beads, pebbles, shot or seeds. Normally played in pairs.

### marching machine

An instrument which consists of a wooden frame with blocks of wood that are loosely attached by means of wire or string. The blocks of wood are struck against a hard surface while the performer holds onto the frame thus producing the effect of marching feet. See picture #66.

### marimba

A keyboard instrument which consists of bars made out of honduras rosewood or a synthetic material that are suspended over metal resonators which are encased in a frame. The timbre of the instrument is a mellow sound. The standard range is 4-4⅓ octaves. Played with rubber or yarn mallets.

### marimba gong

An obsolete instrument that has been replaced by the vibraphone of today without the use of the motor. Also known as a *mettalophone*.

### marimba-xylophone

A keyboard instrument which consists of bars made out of honduras rosewood or a synthetic material that are suspended over metal resonators which are encased in a frame. The instrument has the full range of the xylophone and marimba. Also known as a *xylomarimba* or *xylorimba*.

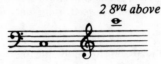

### marimbula

A plucked instrument which consists of pieces of spring steel that are suspended over a sound hole cut out from a wooden box resonator. The instrument can also be played by slapping the box with an open hand.

### mark tree

A set of graduated small brass tubes which are suspended from a wooden board that is attached to a stand. A metal beater or fingers are used to gliss up and down the instrument. See picture #67.

### mechanized klaxon

An automobile horn of the 1920's with a push down mechanism. See picture #63.

### Mercenary Soldiers drum

A wooden shell drum ranging from 20″-30″ in depth and 16″-20″ in diameter with calf skin heads placed on narrow wooden hoops. Four to six gut strings lie across the bottom head. The drum is equipped with three adjustable legs which enable the drum to stand off the ground. The timbre of the drum is that of a dark, muffled sound. Also known as a *long drum*.

### metal block

A term that can mean either cowbell or anvil.

### metal cabasa

The contemporary version of an afuche which consists of a set of metal beads loosely wrapped around a serrated metal cylinder. It is played by turning the instrument with one hand while resting the beads in the palm of the other hand. Also known as a *cabasa* or *cockolo*. See picture #21.

### metal castanets

Small cymbals about 2″ in diameter that can either be held between the thumb and forefinger, one in each hand, or mounted on tongs or spring board. Normally played in pairs by striking the edges together or by striking the underside of each cymbal together. When mounted, they are known as cymbal tongs or mounted metal castanets. Also known as *finger cymbals*. See picture #107.

### metal disks

Round steel plates or disks that normally range up to 8″ in diameter, be as thick as 1³⁄₁₆″ and weigh as much as 11 lbs. These disks can either be mounted on felt supports or suspended. They are struck with metal beaters. Also known as *steel disks* or *steel plates*.

### metal drum

A circular, heavy metal plate made out of bronze with deep curved rims and a flat ornamented surface. It is suspended and played with beaters made out of felt or cloth. Also known as a *drum gong, kettle gong* or *tam tam*. See picture #85.

### metal log drum

A large wooden box which is partitioned into small sections that act as resonators. One end of the box is open exposing the different resonators. Over these resonators are attached metal plates of different pitches. The range depends upon how many partitions are built into the box. The instrument is played with soft felt or yarn mallets. *Also known as a loo-jon or lujon.*

**metal rasp**
A metal ratchet that simulates the sound of a roulette wheel.

**metal rattle**
A metal container that is filled with pebbles, equipped with a handle, and normally played in pairs. Also known as a *tin horn* or *tin rattle.*

**metal scraper**
A metal container with grooves which are scraped with a metal rod.

**metal shaker**
A cylindrical metal tube filled with beads, pebbles, shots or seeds that is played by shaking the tube back and forth. Also known as a *chocallo, metal tube, metal tube shaker* or *tubo. See picture #35.*

**metal tube. See metal shaker.**

**metal tube shaker. See metal shaker.**

**metal wind chimes**
Suspended pieces of metal, usually tubular, that strike against each other when shaken.

**mettalophone**
An obsolete instrument that has been replaced by today's vibraphone, used without the motor. Also known as a *marimba gong.*

**Mexican beans**
Dried out bean pods about 12″ long with seeds inside that serves as a rattle when shaken. Also known as *pod rattles* or *pod shakers.* See picture #68.

**military snare drum**
A snare drum which normally ranges between 9″-12″ in depth and 15″ in diameter with gut or metal snares. The drum should produce a crisp and dry timbre. Also known as a *field drum.*

**mirdangam**
A South Indian two headed wooden drum. The heads are held in place by hoops that are laced together by leather straps. The head on the right side has three layers of skin with a black paste in the center that gives the drum its tone. The left side has two layers of skin with a different type of paste that is not permanent which enables the head to sound an octave below the right side. Both heads are tuned with wooden blocks. Also known as a *mridanga.* See picture #69.

**mission bell tree**
Small bells that are hung over a bamboo frame and shaken. See picture #70.

**mokubio**
A drum made out of camphor wood and shaped like a disk with a circular cut in the bottom that acts as a resonator. A very short raised disk is located on top which is where the drum is struck. The drum stands on three short wooden legs that are attached to the bottom. The mallets can be xylophone mallets or mallets made of hardwood. The sound is similar to a temple block.. Also known as a *Chinese wooden drum, Japanese wood block, Japanese wooden drum* or *mokugyo.*

**mokugyo. See mokubio.**

**monkey drum**
a small hour-glass shaped drum with string tension heads and one or two knotted cords that are attached to the center of the drum. Played with quick turns of the wrist causing the cords to strike the heads. Also known as a *rattle drum.* See picture #76.

**motor horns**
Any mechanism that can duplicate the sound of an automobile horn. Also known as an *auto horn, bulb horn, car horn* or *taxi horn.* See picture #94.

**mounted castanets**
A pair of hollow, circular wooden clappers, mounted on a board and spring tensioned. See picture #101.

### mounted finger cymbals

Small cymbals about 2″ in diameter that are played in pairs and clapped together. Can be mounted on tongs or mounted on a board with spring tension. Also known as *mounted metal castanets.*

### mounted metal castanets. *See mounted finger cymbals.*

### mouth siren

A cylindrical metal whistle which, when blown into, causes a disk inside to rotate and produce a howling glissando effect. Also known as a *cyclone whistle* or *siren whistle.* See picture #42.

### mridanga

A South Indian two headed wooden drum. The heads are held in place by hoops that are laced together by leather straps. The head on the right side has three layers of skin with a black paste in the center that gives the drum its tone. The left side has two layers of skin with a different type of paste that is not permanent which enables the head to sound an octave below the right side. Both heads are tuned with wooden blocks. Also known as a *mirdangam.* See picture #69.

### multiple whips

Several wooden boards or clappers which are struck together at the same time or in an alternating manner. See picture #71.

### musical glasses

A set of drinking glasses tuned by filling with water to different levels and struck with a light wooden beater or rubbed with a moistened finger. The glasses can be arranged to produce an entire scale. The glasses should sit on a cloth. Also known as *cup glasses, glass harp* or *tuned glasses.*

### musical saw

A saw which is played by using a bass or cello bow or by being struck with a mallet. The pitch is changed by bending the bladé as it is being bowed or struck. See picture #72.

# N

### nabimba

A marimba which has small skins placed inside the resonators to produce a buzzing effect. Also known as a *buzz marimba.*

### nightingale

A whistle which, when partially filled with water and blown into, produces the sounds of birds. See picture #112.

### nipple gong

A round, heavy bronze plate of definite pitch with a raised boss or nipple in the center. The instrument is struck on the raised boss or nipple with a felt or cloth covered mallet. Different sizes will produce different pitches. Also known as a *button gong, domed gong* or *gong.* See picture #47.

# O

### octabans

A series of eight elongated, cylindrical, single headed drums that are tuned diatonically. They are made out of fibre shells.

### o-daiko

A large two headed suspended barrel drum of Japan. The heads are made of cowhide and are nailed to the wooden shell with a great deal of tension. The size of the drum is 32″-40″ in diameter and up to 40″ wide. The drum is played with felt beaters or round wooden sticks. A special effect can be created by scraping the nails with the stick.

### oil drum

The top of an empty oil drum in which are hammered various grooves of different sizes and shapes that produce a certain pitch. The drum is played with rubber tipped or padded mallets. The drum is either mounted on a frame or suspended from the performer's neck. Also known as a *steel drum*. See picture #73.

### orchestra bells

A 2½ octave mallet instrument made out of steel bars, usually without resonators. The bells are encased in a wooden box and suspended by soft strings. Some sets of orchestra bells are equipped with a damper mechanism. Brass, hard rubber or hard plastic mallets are used.

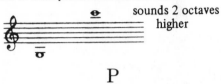

sounds 2 octaves higher

## P

### Pakistan tree bells

A series of cup shaped bells mounted on a single rod in graduating sizes. Played with a brass mallet in a glissando fashion. Also known as a *bell tree*. See picture #14.

### pandereta Brasileno

A rectangular bamboo frame made out of bamboo sticks with a handle and two rows of tambourine jingles. Played by beating the frame against the palm of the hand.

### parade drum

A smaller version of the long drum. The drum has a wood, metal or brass shell with calf heads. The average size is 16″ × 16″. There are 4-6 gut strings that lie across the bottom head. The drum can either stand off the ground using the three adjustable legs or mounted on a stand.

### Parsifal bells

A name used to designate orchestra bells made by Deagan from 1918-32. The uniqueness of these bells was that the set had resonators and its own folding stand.

### Parsifal chimes

Eight chimes that range from E below middle C to B just below middle C. Also known as *bass chimes*.

### pasteboard rattle

A small cylindrical shell of metal or wood approximately 3″ wide and 2⅛″ deep covered with a calfskin head. A small hole is cut into the center of the head through which a gut string is placed. One end of the string is tied to the underside of the head while the other end is looped around a rosined groove in a wooden handle. Holding one end of the handle, the player whirls the instrument around in the air causing the string to slide around the groove of the handle thereby creating vibrations. The vibrations are transmitted to the skin to produce a roaring sound. Due to the fact that performance of this instrument in this manner requires a great deal of room, a more practical method is to place the shell inbetween the knees of the player. The handle has been fitted with cranks that have been attached to both ends. By rotating the cranks with both hands and keeping the string taut the same effect can be created. Different dynamics and timbre can be created by variations in the speed of the rotation and tension of the string.

### pavillon

A stick with a metal top in the shape of a crescent with other ornaments and symbols from which small bells and jingles are suspended. The instrument is played by shaking the stick or striking the stick on the floor. Also known as a *hat, jingling Johnnie or Turkish crescent*.

### pea whistle

A whistle, that when blown into, activates a small ball which produces a loud, high, shrill sound. Also known as a *police whistle*. See picture #113.

### pedal cymbal

Two cymbals mounted on a metal rod operated by a foot mechanism which brings the two cymbals together. Also known as a *charleston, foot cymbal, high hat, hi-hat or sock cymbal*.

### Persian temple bells

A graduated series of cylindrical or conical shaped iron bells. They are attached to a rope, one inside each other, or suspended individually in a row and shaken. Also known as *camel bells*. See picture #22.

### piccolo snare drum

A small snare drum the size of which is approximately 3″×13″. The sound is thinner in timbre and higher in pitch than other snare drums.

### piccolo timpany

Drums made out of copper bowls shaped like kettles that produce definite pitches. The drums are single headed and usually equipped with a foot pedal for tuning changes. The drums are any size under 20″ in diameter. The instrument is played with felt mallets of different hardnesses.

### pistol shot

A sound produced by a pistol firing blanks. Also known as a *revolver* or *starter's pistol*. See picture #117.

### plates

A pair of cymbals equipped with leather straps that are struck together. Also known as *crash cymbals* or *hand cymbals* when indicated in a symphonic setting.

### plate bells

Flat suspended pieces of metal which are struck with a metal hammer. Can be of definite or indefinite pitch. Also known as *bell plates*. See picture #97.

### pod rattle

A dried out bean pod about 12″ long with seeds inside that serves as a rattle when shaken. Also known as *Mexican beans* or *pod shakers*. See picture #68.

### pod shaker. *See* pod rattle.

### police siren

An instrument which is hand cranked or electric. The sound is produced when a perforated rotating disk interrupts the flow of air creating an ascending and descending glissando effect. The instrument may be equipped with an additional crank that enables the performer to stop the sound immediately. Also known as an *air-raid siren, siren* or *warning siren*.

### police whistle

A whistle that, when blown into, activates a small ball which produces a loud, high, shrill sound. Also known as a *pea whistle*. See picture #113.

### pop gun

A long, hollow, cylindrical metal tube with a cork at the one end that is attached to a suction handle at the other end. The cork is sucked into the tube when the handle is pulled back, and popped out when the handle is pressed forward, thus creating a "pop" effect. See picture #74.

### prayer bell

A cup shaped bell which rests on a cushion and is played on the inner rim with a leather, rubber or cloth covered mallet. Also known as a *Buddha temple bell, Japanese temple bell, temple cup bell, dobaci, temple cup gong, cup gong, temple bell, cup bell* or *dabachi*. See picture #18.

### prayer stones

Any two flat stones in which the edge of one is used to strike the surface of the other. They are 2″-3″ in diameter. Also known as *stones* or *Tibetan prayer stones*.

### puili sticks

Bamboo sticks from Hawaii that are played by striking each other, striking the tubes against the body, or by shaking the sticks. See picture #75.

# Q

### quail call

A whistle with a slide at one end which produces the sound of a quail when short breaths of air are blown while at the same time pulling the slide in and out.

**quinto**

The smallest of the conga drums. It is a single headed, elongated barrel or conical shell which is approximately 11″ in diameter. The drum is equipped with tension rods and is normally played with the hands.

# R

**rain machine**

A large barrel made of wood and screen wire which revolves. Inside the barrel are small pebbles which tumble when the barrel is in motion to produce the sound of rain.

**rasp**

Any object that has a notched surface that can be scraped with a stick, i.e. guiro. See picture #56.

**rasper**

A scraped instrument used in Latin America music. It is a hollowed out calabash with notches cut into the upper body and scraped with a stick. *Also known as a gourd, gourd scraper, guiro, rasp, rasping stick, scraper, scratcher, wood scraper or wooden scratcher.* See picture #56.

**rasping stick.** *See rasper.*

**ratchet**

An instrument that reproduces the sound effect of a stick running along a picket fence. *Also known as a cog rattle.* See picture #38.

**rattle**

Any device that is hollow, filled with small objects, and shaken.

**rattle drum**

There are two types of rattle drums. One is a two headed drum with a handle. A knotted cord is attached to the rim of each head. The drum is played with quick turns of the wrist causing the cords to strike the heads. This is also known as a *Chinese hand drum, Chinese paper drum or snake dance rattle.* See picture #30. The second type of drum is a small hour-glass shaped drum with string tension heads and one or two knotted cords that are attached to the center of the drum. Played with quick turns of the wrist causing the cords to strike the heads. Also known as a *monkey drum.* See picture #76.

**revolver**

A sound produced by a pistol firing blanks. Also known as a *pistol shot* or *starter's pistol.* See picture #117.

**ride cymbal**

A non-pitched metal plate which normally ranges from 18″-22″ in diameter and is suspended.

**ring chime**

A small circular plate made out of polished brass alloy that is placed through the finger and struck with a metal beater.

**rivet cymbal**

A cymbal with several small holes drilled around the outer edge. Small metal rivets are loosely inserted through each hole. Also known as a *sizzle cymbal.* See picture #77.

**roto toms**

Single headed drums without shells and of different sizes which are tuned by rotating the heads with the hand or by a pedal mechanism. See picture #78.

**row rattles**

A series of suspended, small, hard objects such as fruit husks, small shells, animal teeth, etc., that are attached to any type of frame.

# S

**sake barrel**

A wooden barrel about 24″ high that is held together with braided natural fibers rather than with glue or nails. Played with round wooden sticks about 17³⁄₁₆″ long and 1³⁄₁₆″ wide. The drum produces a dark sound. Also known as a *wooden barrel*.

**samba whistle**

A whistle with three individual tones capable of producing any combination of those tones. See picture #114.

**sanctus bells**

Three or four steel bells which are attached to a metal crossbar and shaken. Usually played in pairs.

**sand (paper) blocks**

Two hand held objects covered with sandpaper which are rubbed together.

**sand box**

A rattle made out of tin that is filled with fine grained sand. Also known as a *sand rattle*.

**sand rattle. *See* sand box.**

**sanza**

A series of tuned metal tongues that are attached to a wooden box over a sound hole. The instrument is played by plucking the tongues. Also known as a *kalimba* or *thumb piano. See picture #61.*

***sarna bells***

*Spherical shaped bells made out of brass alloy. The open bottom consists of claw-like pointed prongs and inside a clapper is attached. The diameter ranges from ¾″-4″. Also known as elephant bells.*

**saw blade bells**

Circular saw blades which produce a high sustaining tone. Played with a metal beater.

**scraper**

Any object that has a notched surface that can be scraped with a stick, i.e. guiro. See picture #56.

**scratcher. *See* scraper.**

**service bell**

A small bell which produces a single tone used in hotel lobbies to call for service. Also known as a *finger bell* or *tap bell.* See picture #49.

**shake drum**

A two headed drum, with or without handles, that is filled with pebbles and shaken.

**shaker**

Any rattle or container that is filled with small objects such as seeds, pebbles, sand, etc., that is shaken to produce a sound.

**shekere**

A large gourd that is covered with a net of beads and played by holding the beads still while rotating the gourd, striking the bottom of the gourd against the palm of the hand, or by shaking the gourd.

**shell wind chimes**

Suspended pieces of sea shells that strike against each other when shaken.

**ship's bell**

A cast bronze bell equipped with a metal clapper. The clapper is pulled against the inside of the bell by a leather strap or rope which is attached to the end of the clapper. This bell can be of any size. Also known as an *alarm bell* or *storm bell.* See picture #4.

### ship's whistle

A whistle which is made out of three wooden or metal pipes each having a different pitch. They are attached to each other, but are blown through one mouthpiece. The sound is usually low pitched. Also known as a *fog horn* or *steamboat whistle*. See picture #118.

### side drum

A two headed drum with metal or gut snares that lie across the bottom head. These snares are attached to a lever mechanism on the side of the drum that engages or disengages the snares. The shell is made out of metal or wood and the heads can be made out of calf, plastic or other synthetic material. The drum can be one of many sizes. Also known as a *snare drum*.

### signal whistle

A whistle that is made out of metal or wood tubes about 2"-4" long that can come singly or in twos or threes, attached together, and blown through one mouthpiece creating one, two or three pitches. A single whistle can sometimes be equipped with a finger hole which enables the performer to produce two different pitches.

### siren

An instrument which is hand cranked or electric. The sound is produced when a perforated rotating disk interrupts the flow of air creating an ascending and descending glissando effect. The instrument may be equipped with an additional crank that enables the performer to stop the sound immediately. Also known as an *air-raid siren, police siren* or *warning siren*.

### siren whistle

A cylindrical metal whistle which, when blown into, causes a disk inside to rotate and produce a howling glissando effect. Also known as a *cyclone whistle* or *mouth siren*. See picture #42.

### sistrum

A metal rattle with two or three crossbars. On each crossbar, 3-6 small circular disks of bronze alloy are suspended. The instrument is shaken back and forth, causing the disks to hit each other as well as striking both inner walls of the frame. See picture #80.

### six tone slit drum

A drum made out of a log which is cut in six different sections to produce six high pitched tones. See picture #81.

### sizzle cymbal

A cymbal with several small holes drilled around the outer edge. Small metal rivets are inserted loosely through each hole. Also known as a *rivet cymbal*. See picture #77.

### slap stick

Two rectangular pieces of wood struck together. Both pieces are connected together by a hinge at one end. The length and width can be of any size. Also known as *board clappers, whip* or *wooden clapper*. See picture #82.

### sleigh bells

A set of non-pitched small bells which are attached to a handle or strap and shaken or struck. Also known as *harness bells*. See picture #115.

### slide whistle

A whistle made out of a long tube with a slide at one end. An ascending and descending glissando is produced by moving the slide back and forth while blowing into the mouthpiece. Also known as a *lotus flute, song whistle, swanee piccolo* or *swanee whistle*. See picture #116.

### slit drum

A drum made from the trunk of a tree that is hollowed out with length-wise cuts to produce two pitches and a resonating chamber. Two different tones can be produced by playing at the edge or rim. Played with hard wood sticks or small clubs. Also known as an *African slit drum*. See picture #83.

### snake dance rattle

A two headed drum with a handle. Attached to the rim of each head is a knotted cord. The drum is played with quick turns of the wrist causing the cords to strike the heads. Also known as a *Chinese hand drum, Chinese paper drum* or *rattle drum*. See picture #30.

### snare drum

A two headed drum with metal or gut snares that lie across the bottom head. These snares are attached to a lever mechanism on the side of the drum that engages or disengages the snares. The shell is made out of wood or metal and the heads are made out of calf, plastic or other synthetic materials. The drum can be one of many sizes. Also known as a side drum.

### sock cymbal

Two cymbals mounted on a metal rod operated by a foot mechanism which brings the two cymbals together. Also known as a *charleston, foot cymbal, high hat, hi-hat* or *pedal cymbal.*

### song bells

Metal bars, arranged in a keyboard fashion, with resonators. Played with hard mallets. Sounds one octave lower than orchestra bells.

### song whistle

A whistle made out of a long tube with a slide at one end. An ascending and descending glissando is produced by moving the slide back and forth while blowing into the mouthpiece. Also known as a *lotus flute, slide whistle, swanee piccolo* or *swanee whistle.* See picture #116.

### Spanish tambourine

A tambourine with jingles that are shaped in a rippled form.

### spoons

Two spoons that are held in such a manner that the back of each spoon faces each other. They are played by slapping the spoons between the hand and leg. Some sets have the handles attached to each other. See picture #119.

### spring quiro

A metal tube with a bell shaped opening on which three tunable springs are mounted. When the springs are scraped, various sounds can be created by holding the opened end close to or away from the body.

### spurs

Small metal disks that are mounted on a metal rod that is attached to a handle and shaken.

### square cymbals

A pair of square cymbals, 6"-8" in size, mounted on tongs.

### stamping tubes

Wooden or bamboo tubes which are tuned and played by beating out rhythms on the ground.

### starter's pistol

A sound produced by a pistol firing blanks. Also known as a *pistol shot* or *revolver.* See picture #117.

### steamboat whistle

A whistle which is made out of three wooden or metal pipes each having a different pitch. They are attached to each other, but are blown through one mouthpiece. The sound is usually low pitched. Also known as a *fog horn* or *ship's whistle.* See picture #118.

### steel disks

Round steel plates or disks that can range up to 8" in diameter, be as thick as 1³⁄₁₆" and weigh as much as 11 lbs. These disks can either be mounted on felt supports or suspended. They are struck with metal beaters. Also known as *metal disks* or *steel plates.*

### steel drum

The top of an empty oil drum in which are hammered various grooves of different sizes and shapes each of which produces a certain pitch. The drum is played with rubber tipped or padded mallets. The drum is either mounted on a frame or suspended from the performer's neck. Also known as an *oil drum.* See picture #73.

### steel plates

Round steel plates or disks that can range up to 8″ in diameter, be as thick as 1 3/16″ and weigh as much as 11 lbs. These disks can either be mounted on felt supports or suspended. They are struck with metal beaters. Also known as *metal disks* or *steel disks*.

### steeple bells

Large bronze bells with clappers that are found in church towers. If not available, chimes may be substituted. Also known as *carillon, cast bells* or *church bells.* See picture #23.

### stick rattle

A rattle with a bar or ring onto which any type of rattling object may be strung.

### stones

Any two flat stones in which the edge of one is used to strike the surface of the other. They are 2″-3″ in diameter. Also known as *prayer stones* or *Tibetan prayer stones.*

### stone chimes

A keyboard instrument the bars of which are made out of stone disks and played with a hard hammer. Also known as a *lithophone* or *stone disks.*

### stone disks. *See stone chimes.*

### storm bell

A cast bronze bell equipped with a metal clapper. The clapper is pulled against the inside of the bell by a leather strap or rope which is attached to the end of the clapper. This bell can be of any size. Also known as an *alarm bell* or *ship's bell.* See picture #4.

### straw xylophone

A xylophone in which the bars are separated by straw.

### string drum

A drum which is made out of a cylindrical piece of wood or metal one opening of which is covered with a skin. In the center of the skin is a small hole through which a gut string protrudes. A moistened or rosined piece of leather or canvas is pulled along the string away from the drum producing the sound of a lion's roar. The smaller version is known as a dog's bark. Also known as a *jackdaw* or *lion's roar.* See picture #108.

### strung clapper

A series of small boards strung together with handles at each end. Played with a whip like motion to simulate the sound of a row of falling dominos. Also known as a *bin zasara.* See picture #15.

### strung rattle

Small objects such as seeds, shells, etc., that are strung together on cords or tied together in bundles and used as a rattle.

### suspended cymbal

Any size cymbal that is suspended on a stand. The cymbal can be played with any type of beater.

### swanee piccolo

A whistle made out of a long tube with a slide at one end. An ascending and descending glissando is produced by moving the slide back and forth while blowing into the mouthpiece. Also known as a *lotus flute, slide whistle* or *swanee whistle.* See picture #116.

### swanee whistle. *See swanee piccolo.*

### switch

A bunch of twigs attached to a handle and played on the shell of a bass drum. See picture #75.

# T

### tabla

A high sounding, one headed drum made out of wood. The head is made in three sections. A black patch is pasted to the head a little off center with a second skin approximately 1″ in width which runs around the outer circumference of the drumhead. The drum is played with the fingers and hand striking the various surfaces of the drum. See picture #84.

### tabor

The authors have found a great deal of confusion concerning this term. Depending upon the geographical location and historical time, this drum can have one or two heads, come with or without snares, and have the snares placed either on the snare head or batter head. It is the author's opinion that due to this confusion, the type of drum that should be used is a long drum without snares.

### taiko

A wooden shell drum approximately 6⅜″ x 13⅝″ with horse or cowhide heads that is rope tensioned by thick heavy cords. Extreme tension is used to produce a bright, penetrating, crackling sound. Played with round wooden sticks.

### talking drum

A two headed drum with an hour glass shape that is held under one arm. Pitch is changed when the ropes that connect the two heads are squeezed. Also known as an *African goblet drum*. See picture #1.

### tambourine

A narrow, wooden shell drum with or without a head. Around the shell are openings in which small metal disks are mounted in pairs. Played by shaking the instrument or by striking the head or shell.

### tam tam

A circular, heavy metal plate made out of bronze with deep curved rims and a flat ornamented surface. It is suspended and played with beaters made out of felt or cloth. Also known as a *drum gong, kettle gong* or *metal drum*. See picture #85.

### tapan

A two headed rope tensioned drum that can be considered as a small bass drum or very large tenor drum. Played vertically like a bass drum and struck with a felt or cloth covered flat edged beater. Also known as a *tupan*.

### tap bell

A small bell which produces a single tone used in hotel lobbies to call for service. Also known as a *finger bell* or *service bell*. See picture #49.

### tap box

A rectangular block of wood with a horizontal slit near both playing surfaces which serves as a sound chamber. Played with a wooden stick or hard rubber mallet. Also known as a *clog box* or *wood block*.

### tarbourka

A goblet shaped hand held drum made out of clay or metal with sheepskin heads that are tightened by strings or tension rods. The drum is played with the fingers or open palm in both the center and edge of the head. Also known as an *Arabian hand drum, derabucca, doumbek, dumbek* or *dumbeg*. See pictures #9 & 45.

### taxi horn

A conical shaped metal tube with a bulb at one end. Played by squeezing the bulb, producing the sound of a car horn. Also known as an *auto horn, bulb horn, car horn* or *motor horn*. See picture #94.

### tchanchiki

A small Japanese gong in the shape of a pot. The outer edge is grooved and serves as the beating spot. Played with a beater made out of horn.

### temple bell

A cup shaped bell which rests on a cushion and is played on the inner rim with a leather, rubber or cloth covered mallet. Also known as a *Buddha temple bell, Japanese temple bell, prayer bell, temple cup bell, dobaci, temple cup gong, cup gong, cup bell* or *dabachi*. See picture #18.

### temple blocks

A series of five rounded or squared blocks of wood that are hollowed out and struck with a soft mallet. Traditionally tuned to a pentatonic scale. Also known as *Chinese temple blocks, dragon's mouths, fish drums, Korean blocks* or *wooden fish*. See picture #31.

### temple cup bell

A cup shaped bell which rests on a cushion and is played on the inner rim with a leather, rubber or cloth covered mallet. Also known as a *Buddha temple bell, Japanese temple bell, prayer bell, dobaci, temple cup gong, cup gong, temple bell, cup bell* or *dabachi*. See picture #18.

### temple cup gong. *See* temple cup bell.

### tenor drum

A two headed wooden shell drum without snares. The size ranges from 12"-16" in depth and 14"-18" wide.

### Thailand tree bells

A series of cup shaped bells mounted on a single rod in graduating sizes. Played with a brass mallet in a glissando fashion. Also known as a *bell tree*. See picture #14.

### thick plates

Depending on how the part is written, this term can mean either crash cymbals or antique cymbals. If a pitch is indicated in the part, the part is to be played on antique cymbals. If no pitch is indicated, the part is to be played with crash cymbals.

### thumb piano

A series of tuned metal tongues that are attached to a wooden box over a sound hole. The instrument is played by plucking the tongues. Also known as a *kalimba* or *sanza*. See picture #61.

### thunder sheet

A large, thin, suspended sheet of metal that produces the sound of thunder when shaken. Also known as a *foil rattle*.

### thunder stick

A thin piece of wood attached to a string which is whirled in the air producing a howling sound. The faster the instrument is whirled the higher the pitch. Also known as a *bull roarer* or *whizzer*. See picture #19.

### Tibetan prayer stones

Any two flat stones in which the edge of one is used to strike the surface of the other. They are 2"-3" in diameter. Also known as *prayer stones* or *stones*.

### timbales

A pair of one headed cylindrical drums mounted on a stand. The shells are made out of metal. The drums are tensioned a perfect 4th or 5th apart and played with long thin wooden sticks. See picture #86.

### timpany

A drum made out of copper or fiberglass bowls shaped like kettles that produce definite pitches. The drums are single headed and usually equipped with a foot pedal for tuning changes. The drums are played with felt mallets of different hardness. Also known as *kettle drums*.

### tin horn

A metal container that is filled with pebbles, equipped with a handle and normally played in pairs. Also known as a *metal rattle* or *tin rattle*.

### tin rattle. *See* tin horn.

### tom tom

A single or two headed drum, of any size, without snares.

### train whistle

A whistle which is made out of three wooden or metal pipes each having a different pitch. They are attached to each other, but are blown through one mouthpiece. The sound is high in pitch. See picture #118.

### trap set

A standard set of drums which includes a snare drum, tom toms (both mounted and floor tom tom), a pedaled bass drum, hi-hat and any number of suspended cymbals. Played by one person. Also known as a *drum set*.

### tree cymbals

A graduated series of suspended cymbals placed one on top of each other on a stand. Normally played with a metal beater in a glissando fashion. Also known as a *cymbal tree*.

### triangle

A piece of steel rod bent in the shape of a triangle with one corner opened. Suspended on a thin cord that is attached to a clamp. Played with a metal beater.

### trip gong

A bowl shaped bell made out of brass that is played with a hammer on the side of the bell. Also known as a *fire bell* or *fighter's bell*. See picture #48.

### trough xylophone

A set of wooden bars placed in a single row, either diatonically or chromatically, over a long narrow curved box that acts as a resonator. Played with mallets of felt, rubber or wooden heads. See picture #87.

### tubaphone

A set of brass or steel tubes about 5/8″ in diameter arranged in a keyboard fashion. Played with spoon-like wooden mallets that are padded with leather to get a metallic, hollow sound. The tubes can produce a slight vibrato effect by being suspended on thin cords.

sounds 2 octaves higher

### tubo

A cylindrical metal tube filled with beads, pebbles, shot or seeds that is played by shaking the tube back and forth. Also known as a *chocallo*, *metal shaker*, *metal tube* or *metal tube shaker*. See picture #35.

### tubular bells

Normally a 1½ octave set of metal tubes suspended vertically on a frame and played with a rawhide mallet. Extended ranges are available. Also known as *chimes* or *tubular chimes*.

### tubular chimes. *See tubular bells.*

### tubular wood block

A two-toned tubular wood block made out of hardwood. Both blocks are partially hollowed out with slits at both openings. Played with a wooden stick. Also known as a *cylindrical wood block* or *wooden agogos*. See picture #43.

### tumbadora

The largest of the conga drums. A single headed, elongated barrel or conical shell drum which is normally played with the hands. The drum is equipped with tension rods. The diameter is 12½″.

### tuned bottles

A series of empty bottles that are arranged by size and pitch on a rack. Each bottle can be fine tuned by adding water. Played with leather padded xylophone mallets.

## tuned glasses

A set of drinking glasses tuned by filling with water to different levels and struck with a light wooden beater or rubbed with a moistened finger. The glasses can be arranged to produce an entire scale. The glasses should sit on a cloth. Also known as *cup glasses, glass harp* or *musical glasses*.

## tuned log

A hollowed out log or wooden rectangular box in which one or more tongues have been cut into the lid. Each tongue produces a different pitch. This instrument is used to imitate the sounds of African slit drums. Also known as *African tree drum, jungle wood drum, log drum* or *wooden gong*. See picture #81.

## tupan

A two headed rope tensioned drum that can be considered as a small bass drum or a large tenor drum. Played vertically like a bass drum and struck with a cloth or felt covered flat edged beater. Also known as a *tapan*.

## Turkish crescent

A stick with a metal top in the shape of a crescent with other ornaments and symbols from which small bells and jingles are suspended. The instrument is played by shaking the stick or pounding on the floor. Also known as a *hat, jingling Johnnie* or *pavillon*.

## Turkish drum

A large two headed drum which is played on both sides. One side is played with a cloth or leather beater on the beat and the other side is played with a switch on the beat or on the afterbeat. This drum is known today a the bass drum.

# V

## Venezualan friction drum

A barrel drum which produces a grunting sound when a rosined cord is pulled through a small opening in the drumhead.

## vessel rattle

A hollowed out calabash filled with pebbles or seeds and shaken by means of a hemp holder. Also known as a *gourd rattle*. See picture #55.

## vibes

A set of metal bars that are arranged in a keyboard fashion and suspended over metal resonators. Equipped with a motor that manipulates small circular metal disks in the resonators that can create a vibrato effect. Also equipped with a pedal that can dampen or sustain the sound. Also known as a *vibraharp* or *vibraphone*.

**Vibraharp.** *See vibes.*

**Vibraphone.** *See vibes.*

## Vibraslap

The contemporary version of the jawbone. This instrument produces a rattling sound by striking the ball of the instrument allowing the small metal pegs at the other end to vibrate inside a wooden sound chamber. See picture #88.

# W

## warning siren

An instrument which is either hand cranked or electric. The sound is produced when a perforated rotating disk interrupts the flow of air, creating an ascending or descending glissando effect. The instrument may be equipped with an additional crank that enables the performer to stop the sound immediately. Also known as an *air-raid siren, police siren* or *siren*.

**wasamba rattle**

A rattle which consists of 10-15 disks cut from fruit husks that are strung on a tree branch and shaken. See picture #89.

**washboard**

A wooden frame with a glass or metal serrated surface which is scraped with a thimble, fingernails or a metal stick. See picture #90.

**water drum**

A large calabash that is cut in half and filled with water. A second, smaller calabash is cut in half and placed in the water with the opened end facing down. The calabash is then struck with an even smaller calabash that is equipped with a handle. Also known as a *water gourd.*

**water gong**

A sound effect which is produced by striking a gong or tam tam and immediately immersing it half way into water, causing a descending glissando. An ascending glissando can be produced in the reverse manner.

**water gourd**

As large calabash that is cut in half and filled with water. A second, smaller calabash is cut in half and placed in the water with the opened end facing down. The calabash is then struck with an even smaller calabash that is equipped with a handle. Also known as a *water drum.*

**waterphone**

A suspended container that has a series of steel prongs extending from its outer edge, and a funnel which is connected through the center so that water can be poured into it. When the steel prongs are struck, bowed or scraped, an eerie sound is produced as the water moves inside the container.

**whip**

Two rectangular pieces of wood struck together. Both pieces are connected together by a hinge at one end. The length and width can be of any size. Also known as *board clappers, slap stick* or *wooden clapper.* See picture #82.

**whizzer**

A thin piece of wood attached to a string which is whirled in the air producing a howling sound. The faster the instrument is whirled the higher the pitch. Also known as a *bull roarer* or *thunder stick.* See picture #19.

**wind chimes**

Any small objects that are suspended which strike against each other when shaken.

**wind machine**

A rotating wooden cylinder that is hand cranked and rests on a rack. Boards are attached to the cylinder which have sharp edges that rub against a heavy canvas which drapes over the cylinder. See picture #91.

**wire coils**

An automobile coilspring that is suspended and struck with a metal beater. Also known as a *coilspring.* See picture #102.

**wood bell**

A maraca shaped wood block with two beaters, one on each side of the block. Played by shaking the block. A series of these bells can be mounted and shaken together. See picture #92.

**wood block**

A rectangular block of wood with a horizontal slit near both playing surfaces which serves as a sound chamber. Played with a wooden stick or hard rubber mallet. Also known as a *clog box* or *tap box.*

**wood drum**

A single headed drum with a thin sheet of wood used as the drumhead instead of a skin. Also known as a *wooden tom tom* or *wood-plate drum.*

## wooden agogo

A two toned tubular wood block made out of hardwood. Both ends are partially hollowed out with slits at both openings. Played with a wooden stick. Also known as a *cylindrical wood block* or *tubular wood block*. See picture #43.

## wooden barrel

A wooden barrel about 24" high that is held together with braided natural fibers rather than glue or nails. Played with round wooden sticks about 17³⁄₁₆" long and 1³⁄₁₆" wide. The drum produces a dark sound. Also known as a *sake barrel*.

## wooden boards

Any size board that is played with round wooden sticks. For different sounds, the board can be struck in the middle or at the edge.

## wooden clapper

Two rectangular pieces of wood struck together. Both pieces are connected together by a hinge at one end. The length and width can be of any size. Also known as *board clappers*, *slap stick*, or *whip*. See picture #82.

## wooden fish

A series of five rounded or squared blocks of wood that are hollowed out and struck with a soft mallet. Traditionally tuned to a pentatonic scale. Also known as *Chinese temple blocks, dragon's mouths, fish drums, Korean blocks* or *temple blocks*. See picture #31.

## wooden gong

A hollowed out log or wooden rectangular box in which one or more tongues have been cut into the lid. Each tongue produces a different pitch. This instrument is used to imitate the sounds of African slit drums. Also known as *African tree drum, jungle wood drum, log drum* or *tuned log*. See picture #81.

## wooden scraper

A scraped instrument used in Latin American music. It is a hollowed out calabash or piece of wood with notches cut into the upper body and scraped with a stick. Also known as a *gourd, gourd scraper, guiro, rasp, rasper, rasping stick, scraper, scratcher* or *wooden scratcher*. See picture #56.

## wooden scratcher. *See wooden scraper.*

## wooden shaker

A cylindrical wooden pipe that is filled with seeds and shaken.

## wooden spoons

Spoons that are made out of hardwood which are held in each hand. They are played by opening and closing the fingers.

## wooden tom tom

A single headed drum with a thin sheet of wood used as the drum head instead of skin. Also known as a *wood drum* or *wood-plate drum*.

## wooden wind chimes

Suspended pieces of bamboo which strike against each other when shaken. Also known as *bamboo wind chimes* or *Japanese wood chimes*. See picture #95.

## wood-plate drum

A single headed drum with a thin sheet of wood used as the drumhead instead of a skin. Also known as a *wood drum* or *wooden tom tom*.

# X

**xylomarimba**

Wooden bars arranged in a keyboard fashion and suspended over resonators that are mounted on a frame. The instrument has the full range of the xylophone and marimba. Also known as a *marimba-xylophone* or *xylorimba*.

**xylophone**

Wooden bars arranged in a keyboard fashion and suspended over resonators that are mounted on a frame. Played with hard rubber or wooden mallets.

**xylorimba.** *See* **xylomarimba.**

# II.
# Photographs
# of the
# Instruments

1. African goblet drum
   Courtesy of Dr. T. Temple Tuttle

4. Ship's bell
   Courtesy of Emil Richards

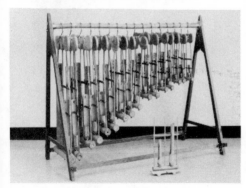

6. Angklungs
   Courtesy of Dr. T. Temple Tuttle

2. Afuche
   Courtesy of Dr. T. Temple Tuttle

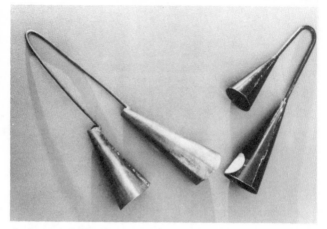

3. Agogo bells
   Courtesy of Thomas Fries

5. Alpine herd cowbells
   Courtesy of the Cleveland Orchestra

44

7. Ankle Bells
   Courtesy of Dr. T. Temple Tuttle

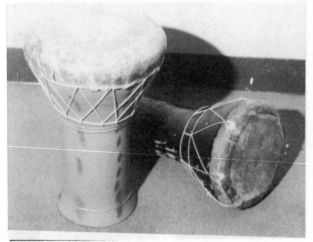

8. Antique cymbals
   Courtesy of the Cleveland Orchestra

9. Arabian hand drum
   Courtesy of Halim El-Dabh

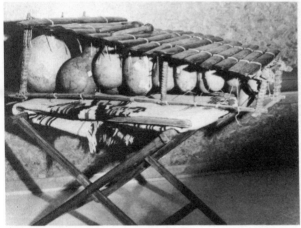

10. Balafon
    Courtesy of Greg Selker

12. Barrel drum
    Courtesy of Terry Miller

11. Bamboo slit log
    Courtesy of Dr. T. Temple Tuttle

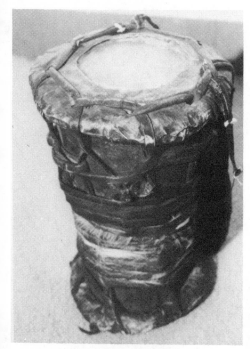

13. Bata drum
    Courtesy of Halim El-Dabh

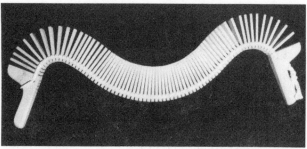

15. Bin zasara
    Courtesy of Frank A. Stolarski

16. Boobams
    Courtesy of Emil Richards

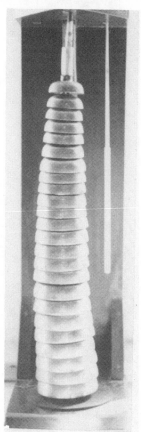

14. Bell tree
    Courtesy of the
    Cleveland Orchestra

17. Brake drums
    Courtesy of the Cleveland Institute
    of Music

18. Buddha temple bell
    Courtesy of
    Emil Richards

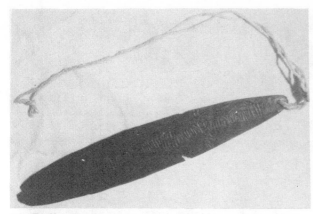

19. Bull roarer
Courtesy of Donald Miller

20. Burma bell
Courtesy of Emil Richards

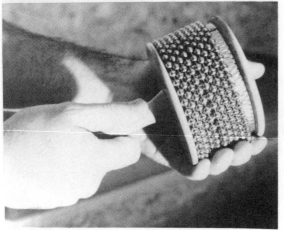

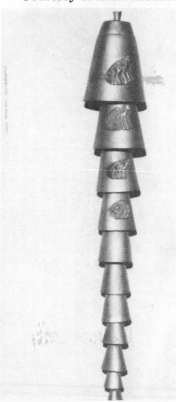

21. Cabasa

22. Camel bells
Courtesy of Donald Miller

23. Carillon
Courtesy of the Church of the Covenant

24. Caxixi
Courtesy of Greg Selker

26. Chinese Confucian bells
Courtesy of Emil Richards

25. Chimta
Courtesy of Dr. T. Temple Tuttle

28. Chinese cymbal

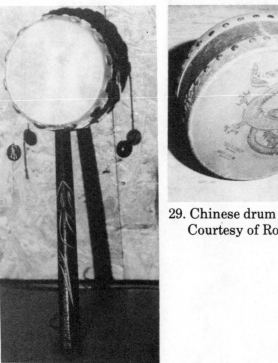

29. Chinese drum
Courtesy of Robert Matson

27. Chinese cup gongs
Courtesy of Greg Selker

30. Chinese hand drum
Courtesy of Greg Selker

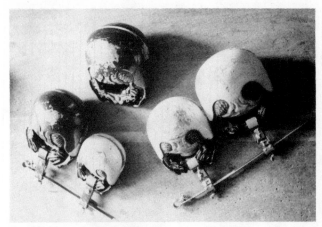

31. Chinese temple blocks
   Courtesy of the Cleveland Orchestra

32. Chinese tom tom
   Courtesy of Terry Miller

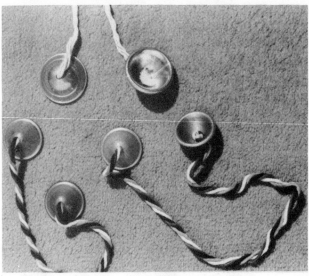

33. Chings
   Courtesy of Terry Miller

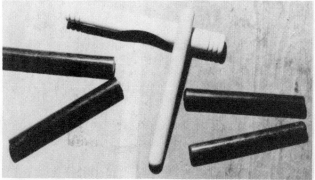

34. Ching-a-ring
   Courtesy of Robert Matson

36. Claves

35. Chocallo
   Courtesy of the Cleveland Orchestra

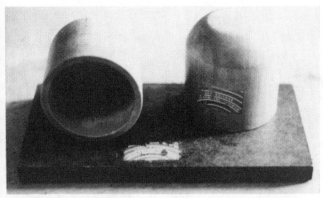

37. Horses hooves
    Courtesy of the Cleveland Orchestra

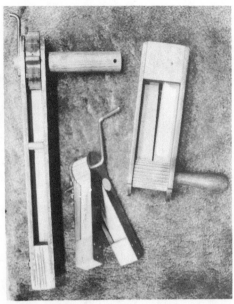

38. Ratchets
    Courtesy of the
    Cleveland Orchestra

39. Concussion blocks
    Courtesy of Halim El-Dabh

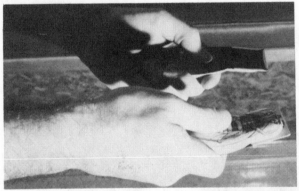

41. Cuica
    Courtesy of Mike Shellenbarger

40. Cricket clickers

42. Siren whistle

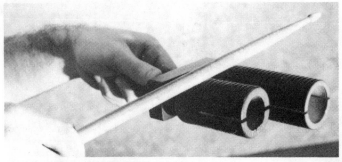

43. Wooden agogos
Courtesy of Academy Music

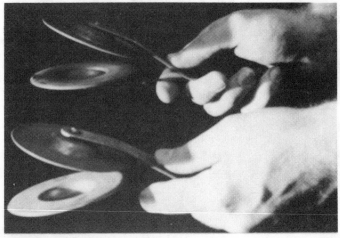

44. Cymbal tongs
Courtesy of Prospect Music

45. Derabucca
Courtesy of
Dr. T. Temple Tuttle

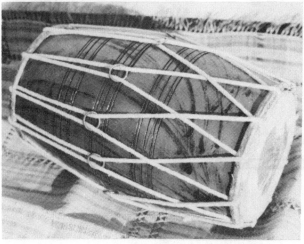

46. Dholak
Courtesy of Dr. T. Temple Tuttle

47. Gongs
Courtesy of the Cleveland Orchestra

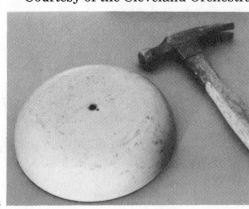

48. Fighter's bell
Courtesy of Thomas Fries

49. Finger bell

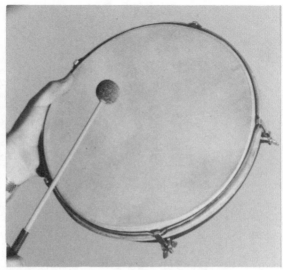

52. Frame drum
     Courtesy of Dr T. Temple Tuttle

50. Flexatone

53. Gamelan gongs
     Courtesy of Halim El-Dabh

54. Goblet drum
     Courtesy of
     Halim El-Dabh

51. Foot bell
     Courtesy of Emil Richards

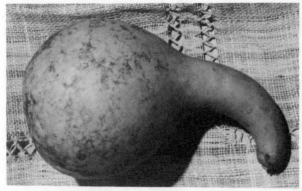

55. Gourd rattle
Courtesy of Dr. T. Temple Tuttle

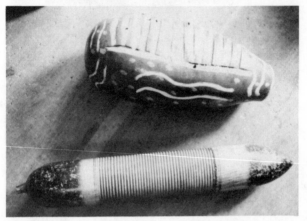

56. Guiro
Courtesy of the Cleveland Orchestra

57. Hour-glass drum
Courtesy of Emil Richards

58. Indian jingles
Courtesy of Dr. T. Temple Tuttle

59. Jawbone (of an ass)
Courtesy of Emil Richards

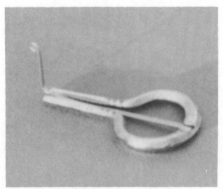

60. Jaw's (Jew's) harp

61. Kalimba
    Courtesy of Dr. T. Temple Tuttle

63. Klaxon horn
    Courtesy of Prospect Music

62. Khartals
    Courtesy of
    Emil Richards

64. Loo-Jon
    Courtesy of Emil Richards

66. Marching machine
    Courtesy of Emil Richards

65. Mandiras
    Courtesy of Dr. T. Temple Tuttle

67. Mark tree

70. Mission bell tree
Courtesy of Emil Richards

68. Mexican beans

69. Mirdangam
Courtesy of Dr. T. Temple Tuttle

72. Musical saw
Courtesy of the
Cleveland Orchestra

71. Multiple whips
Courtesy of
Robert Matson

55

73. Steel drum
    Courtesy of Mike Shellenbarger

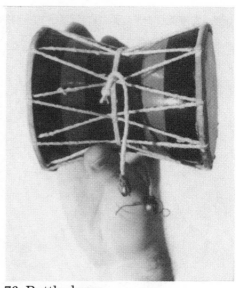

76. Rattle drum
    Courtesy of Dr. T. Temple Tuttle

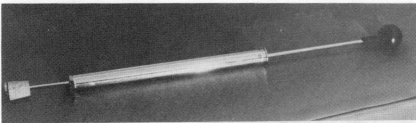

74. Pop gun

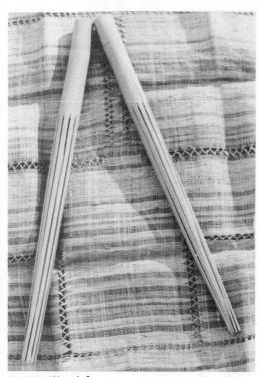

77. Sizzle cymbal

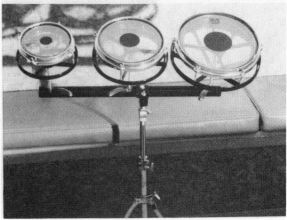

75. Pu ili sticks
    Courtesy of Dr. T. Temple Tuttle

78. Roto toms
    Courtesy of Academy Music

56

79. Shekere
Courtesy of Prospect Music

80. Sistrum
Courtesy of Halim El-Dabh

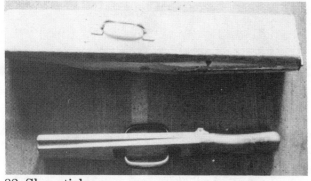

81. Six tone slit drum
Courtesy of Dr. T. Temple Tuttle

84. Tablas
Courtesy of Dr. T. Temple Tuttle

82. Slap stick
Courtesy of the Cleveland Orchestra

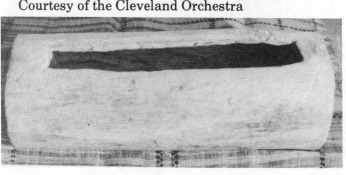

83. Slit drum
Courtesy of
Dr. T. Temple Tuttle

85. Tam Tam
   Courtesy of the Cleveland Orchestra

86. Timbales
   Courtesy of the Cleveland Orchestra

89. Wasamba rattle
   Courtesy of Emil Richards

87. Trough xylophone
   Courtesy of Halim El-Dabh

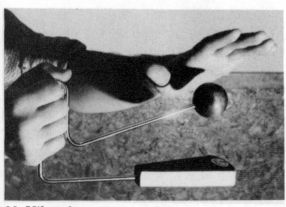

88. Vibraslap

90. Washboard
   Courtesy of the Cleveland Orchestra

91. Wind machine
Courtesy of the Cleveland Orchestra

92. Wood bells
Courtesy of Emil Richards

93. Anvils
Courtesy of the Cleveland Orchestra

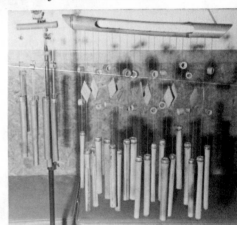

95. Bamboo wind chimes

94. Auto horns
Courtesy of the Cleveland Orchestra

96. Bell lyra
Courtesy of Academy Music

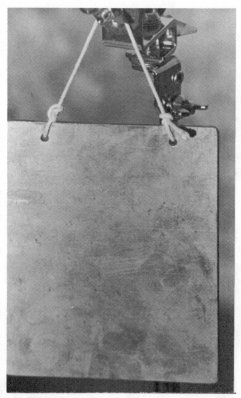

97. Bell plate

99. Bongos

100. Bosuns pipe

101. Mounted castanets

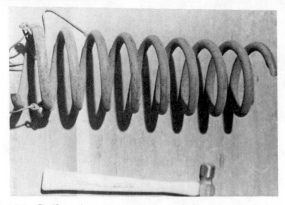

102. Coilspring
    Courtesy of the Cleveland Orchestra

98. Boat whistle
    Courtesy of the Cleveland Orchestra

103. Conga drum

104. Crow call

105. Cuckoo call

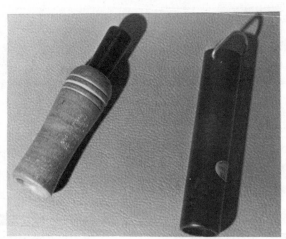

106. Duck call

107. Finger cymbals
Courtesy of Academy Music

108. Lion's roar
and Dog's
bark

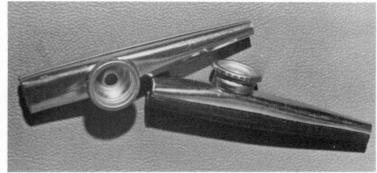

109. Kazoo

110. Key chimes
    Courtesy of
    Academy Music

112. Nightingale

111. Lowboy

113. Police whistles

114. Samba whistle
    Courtesy of Academy Music

115. Sleigh bells

117. Starter's pistol
Courtesy of the Cleveland Orchestra

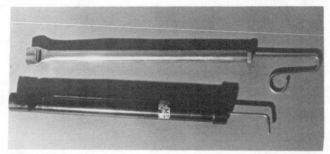

116. Slide whistles

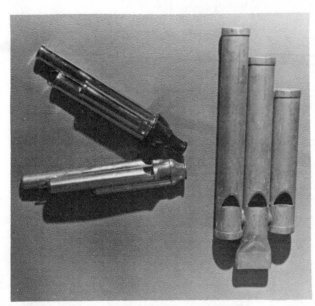

118. Train whistles or Fog horn whistle

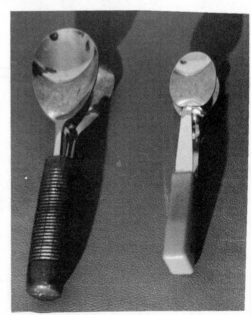

119. Spoons
Courtesy of Thomas Fries

# III.
# Foreign Terms
# and their
# Translations

# A

**acciarino** *(It.)* triangle
**adjá** *(Braz.)* an Afro-Brazilian metal bell
**adufé** *(Braz.)* tambourine
**aeoliphone** *(Ger.)* wind machine
**aeolophon** *(Ger.)* wind machine
**afochê** *(L. Amer.)* cabasa
**Afrikanische harfe** *(Ger.)* marimbula
**Afrikanische schlitztrommel** *(Ger.)* log drum
**Afrikanische schlitztrommeln** *(Ger.)* African slit drums
**afuxé** *(Port.)* cabasa made out of coconut
**aiapá** *(Port.)* shaker
**aidjé** *(Braz.)* a bull roarer or thunder stick
**alarmglocke (n)** *(Ger.)* alarm bell
**l'albero di sonagli** *(It.)* bell tree
**alfandoque** *(Col.)* maracas
**almenglocken** *(Ger.)* Alpine herd cowbells
**almglocken** *(Ger.)* Alpine herd bells
**Alpenglocken** *(Ger.)* Alpine herd cowbells
**ambose** *(Ger.)* anvil
**amboss** *(Ger.)* anvil
**amelé** *(Port.)* rattle
**antike (n) zimbeln** *(Ger.)* antique cymbals
**aolsglocken** *(Ger.)* aeolian bells
**appeau** *(Fr.)* bird whistle
**Arabische trommel** *(Ger.)* Arabian hand drum
**l'arenaiuolo** *(It.)* sandbox
**l'armonica di ventro** *(It.)* glass harmonica
**arpa Africana** *(It.)* marimbula
**assovious** *(Port.)* whistle
**atabal** *(Sp.)* timpany - *(Arab.)* bass drum
**atabales** *(Sp.)* timpany
**atabaloo** *(Sp.)* timpany
**atabaqué** *(Braz.)* Afro-Brazilian drum
**atambor** *(Sp.)* tabor
**autobremstrommeln** *(Ger.)* brake drum
**autohupe** *(Ger.)* automobile horn, taxi horn
**ayochicahuaztli** *(Mex.)* metal rattle

# B

**bacchette di conchiglia sospese** *(It.)* shell wind chimes
**bacchette di legno sospese** *(It.)* wooden wind chimes
**bacchette di metallo sospese** *(It.)* metal wind chimes
**bacchette di ventro sospese** *(It.)* suspended glass wind chimes
**baguettes de bois suspendues** *(Fr.)* wooden wind chimes
**baguettes de coquille suspendues** *(Fr.)* shell wind chimes
**baguettes de verre suspendues** *(Fr.)* suspended glass wind chimes

**baguettes metalliques suspendues** *(Fr.)* metal wind chimes

**balsié tumbado** *(Sant. Dom.)* a low flat one headed drum

**bambou Brésilien** *(Fr.)* Brazilian bamboo shaker

**bambou suspendu** *(Fr.)* suspended bamboo chimes

**bambú...** bamboo wind chimes

**bambu Brasileño** *(Sp.)* Brazilian bamboo scraper

**bambù Brasiliano** *(It.)* Brazilian bamboo shaker

**bambù sospeso** *(It.)* suspended bamboo wind chimes

**bambusraspel** *(Ger.)* bamboo scraper

**bambusrohre** *(Ger.)* bamboo wind chimes

**bambustrommel** *(Ger.)* boobam

**bamya** *(Ger.)* dagga

**bansá** *(Braz.)* an Afro-Brazilian musical bow

**bapó** *(Braz.)* maracas

**baquettes entrechoquées** *(Fr.)* concussion sticks

**baril de bois** *(Fr.)* barrel drum, wooden drum

**baril de sake** *(Fr.)* sake barrel

**barile di legno** *(It.)* barrel drum, wooden drum

**barile di sake** *(It.)* sake barrel

**barra di sospensione con i sonagli** *(It.)* bell tree

**baskettrommel** *(Ger.)* tambourine

**baskische trommel** *(Ger.)* tambourine

**basler trommel** *(Ger.)* parade drum

**basque trommel** *(Ger.)* tambourine

**basse de flandres** *(Fr.)* bumbass

**basstrommel** *(Ger.)* bass drum

**bassxylophon** *(Ger.)* bass xylophone

**batintin** *(Sp.)* nipple gong

**bâton de rythme** *(Fr.)* stamping tube

**batteria** *(It.)* percussion

**batterie** *(Fr.)* percussion

**bechertrommel** *(Ger.)* goblet drum

**becken** *(Ger.)* cymbal

**becken an der grosse trommel befestigt** *(Ger.)* bass drum with cymbal attached

**becken auf ständer** *(Ger.)* suspended cymbal

**becken frei** *(Ger.)* suspended cymbal

**becken hängend** *(Ger.)* suspended cymbal

**becken mit fussmaschine** *(Ger.)* hi-hat

**becken mit teller** *(Ger.)* pair of cymbals, crash cymbals

**becken natürlich** *(Ger.)* crash cymbals

**becken-paar** *(Ger.)* crash cymbals

**becken tambourin** *(Fr.)* tambourine

**becken tambourine** *(Ger.)* tambourine

**beckentrommel** *(Ger.)* tambourine without a head

**beffroi** *(Fr.)* alarm bell

**beinklapper** *(Ger.)* bones

**berra-boi** *(Braz.)* thunder stick

**bhaya** *(Ind.)* dagga

**bicchieri di ventro** *(It.)* tuned glasses

**bin sasara** *(Ger., It., Fr.)* bin zasara

**blechtrommel** *(Ger.)* steel drum

**bloc Chinois** *(Fr.)* Chinese temple blocks

**bloc (s) de bois** *(Fr.)* wood block (s)

**bloc de bois cylindrique** *(Fr.)* tubular wood blocks

**bloc de métal** *(Fr.)* cowbell (without clapper), metal block

**bloc en bois** *(Fr.)* wood block

**blocchi di legno** *(It.)* wood block

**blocchi di legno coreani** *(It.)* Korean blocks

**blocci di legno coreano** *(It.)* Korean blocks

**blocco di legno** *(It.)* wood block

**blocco di legno Cinese** *(It.)* wood block

**blocco di legno coreano** *(It.)* temple blocks

**blocco di metallo** *(It.)* metal block

**block (s) Cinese** *(It.)* temple blocks

**blocks Chinois** *(Fr.)* temple blocks

**blocs a papier di verre** *(Ger.)* sandpaper blocks

**bloques de China** *(Sp.)* Chinese temple blocks

**bloques de madera** *(Sp.)* wood block

**bloques de metal** *(Sp.)* metal block

**bloques de papel de lija** *(Sp.)* sandpaper blocks

**bodhrán...** small frame drum

**bois de madera** *(It.)* wood block

**boite en bois** *(Fr.)* woodblock

**boito à clous** *(Fr.)* maracas

**bol'shói barabán** *(Rus.)* bass drum

**bombo** *(Sp.)* bass drum

**bonghi** *(It.)* bongos

**bongo trommeln** *(Ger.)* bongos

**bongosow** *(Pol.)* bongos

**bottiglie** *(Pol.)* bottles

**bottiglie sospese** *(Pol.)* suspended bottles

**bouteillophon** *(Ger.)* tuned bottles

**bouteillophone** *(Fr.)* tuned bottles

**bremstrommeln von autos** *(Ger.)* brake drums

**brettchenklapper** *(Ger.)* board clappers

**bruit de sonnailles des troupeaux** *(Fr.)* cowbell

**bruit de tôle** *(Fr.)* foil rattle

**brummeisen** *(Ger.)* jaw's (Jew's) harp

**brummtopf** *(Ger.)* friction drum

**bubbolo** *(It.)* jingles

**bubénchik koróv** *(Rus.)* cowbell

**bubentsý** *(Rus.)* jingles

**buckel gong** *(Ger.)* domed gong

**butelki** *(Pol.)* bottles
**buttibu** *(It.)* friction drum
**buttori** *(Braz.)* deer hooves rattle

# C

**cabaca** *(Sp., Port.)* cabasa
**cabaza** *(It.)* cabasa
**caccavella** *(It.)* string drum, friction drum
**cadacada** *(S.A.I.)* shell castanets
**cadonas** *(Sp.)* iron chains
**cairé** *(Braz.)* a cross-shaped rattle
**caisse** *(Fr.)* drum
**caisse à timbre** *(Fr.)* snare drum
**caisse claire** *(Fr.)* snare drum
**caisse claire gr taille** *(Fr.)* large snare drum
**caisse plate** *(Fr.)* piccolo snare drum
**caisse plato** *(Fr.)* piccolo snare drum
**caisse roulant** *(Fr.)* field drum
**caisse roulante** *(Fr.)* tenor drum
**caisse roulante avec cordes** *(Fr.)* field drum
**caisse sourde** *(Fr.)* tom tom
**caisse très claire** *(Fr.)* side drum
**caixa** *(Port.)* military snare drum
**caixa clara** *(Port.)* snare drum
**caixa de campanha** *(L. Amer.)* field drum
**caixa de rufo** *(Port.)* tenor drum
**caixeta** *(Port.)* wood block
**caja** *(Sp.)* snare drum
**caja clara** *(Sp.)* snare drum
**caja rodante** *(Sp.)* tenor drum
**calebasse** *(Fr.)* cabasa
**calypsotrommel** *(Ger.)* steel drum
**camesa** *(Af.)* shaker
**campana d'allarme** *(It.)* alarm bell
**campana da preghiera** *(It.)* prayer bell
**campana di legno** *(It.)* temple block
**campana grave** *(It.)* church bell
**campana in lastra di metallo** *(It.)* bell plate
**campana tubolare** *(It.)* chimes
**campana tubolari** *(It.)* chimes
**campanacci** *(It.)* cowbell
**campanaccio** *(It.)* cowbell
**campanaccio di metallo** *(It.)* cowbell
**campanas** *(Sp.)* orchestra bells
**campanas tubulares** *(Sp.)* chimes
**campanco** *(Sp.)* chimes

campane *(It.)* chimes

campane a lastra d' acciaio *(It.)* plate bells

campane da gregge *(It.)* cowbells

campane da pastore *(It.)* Alpine herd bells

campane de gregge *(It.)* cowbell

campane in lastra di metallo *(It.)* bell plate

campane tibolari *(It.)* chime

campane tubolare *(It.)* chime

campanella *(It.)* small bell

campanelle *(It.)* chimes

campanelle basse *(Fr.)* low bells

campanelle da messa *(It.)* sanctus bells

campanelle de vacca *(It.)* cowbell

campanelle di vacca *(It.)* cowbell

campanelli *(It.)* orchestra bells

campanelli a tastiera *(It.)* orchestra bells

campanelli da mucca *(It.)* cowbell

campanelli giappa *(It.)* orchestra bells

campanelli Giapponese *(It.)* Japanese metal bar(s)

campanello d'allarme *(It.)* alarm bell

campanetta *(It.)* orchestra bells

campanette *(It.)* orchestra bells

campani *(It.)* chimes

campanilla *(Sp.)* hand bells

campanólogo *(Sp.)* orchestra bells

canja rodante *(Sp.)* tenor drum

cannone *(It.)* cannon shot

canon *(Fr.)* cannon shot

canusao *(Port.)* snare drum

cará *(Col.)* maracas

caracachas *(L. Amer.)* scraper

caracaha *(Port.)* quiro

caracalho *(Braz.)* quiro

caracaxá *(Braz.)* wooden scraper

carangano *(Col.)* maracas

cariglione *(It.)* chimes

carillon *(Fr.)* church or steeple bells

carraca *(Sp.)* ratchet, *(Col.)* guiro

carracas *(Mex.)* jingle bells

carrasca *(Col.)* guiro type scraper

carrilhão *(Port.)* orchestra bells

carta sabbiata *(It.)* sandpaper blocks

carta vetrata *(It.)* sandpaper blocks

cascabel *(Sp.)* sleighbells

cascabeles *(Sp.)* bell wheel, *(Mex.)* Mexican Indian pellet bells

cascavels *(L. Amer.)* jingles

cassa *(It.)* drum

**cassa chiara** *(It.)* snare drum

**cassa di legno** *(It.)* wood block

**cassa di metallo** *(It.)* metal block

**cassa grande** *(It.)* bass drum

**cassa piccola** *(It.)* piccolo drum

**cassa rullante** *(It.)* tenor drum

**cassa sordo** *(It.)* military snare drum

**casse chiare** *(It.)* snare drum

**casse di legno** *(It.)* wood block

**cassetta di legno** *(It.)* wood block

**cassettina(e)** *(It.)* wood block

**cassettina di legno** *(It.)* wood block

**castagnetta(e)** *(It.)* castanets

**castagnetta ferra** *(It.)* mounted finger cymbals

**castagnette di ferro** *(It.)* mounted finger cymbals

**castagnetten** *(Ger.)* castanets

**castagnettes** *(Fr.)* castanets

**castagnettes de fer** *(Fr.)* metal castanets

**castañeta(s)** *(Sp.)* castanet(s)

**castanhetas** *(Port.)* castanets

**castanholas** *(Port.)* castanets

**castantes metals** *(Sp.)* mounted finger cymbals

**castañuelas** *(Sp.)* castanets

**catacá** *(Braz.)* Brazilian wooden blocks

**catena(e)** *(It.)* iron chains

**catuba** *(It.)* bass drum

**caxambú** *(Braz.)* bass drum

**cencerro(s)** *(It., Fr., L. Amer.)* cowbell(s)

**ceppi Chinesi** *(It.)* temple blocks

**ceppi Chinosi** *(It.)* temple blocks

**ceppi di carta vetro** *(It.)* sandpaper blocks

**cércol** *(Lat.)* tambourine without the head

**chaghána** *(Turk.)* jingling johnnie

**chaine(s)...**iron chains

**chakra** *(Afr.)* circular wooden castanets

**chanrará** *(Andean)* an Andean jingle rattle

**châpeau Chinois** *(Fr.)* bell tree

**charleston** *(Fr.)* hi-hat

**charleston becken machine** *(Ger.)* hi-hat

**chequeré** *(Braz.)* a double rattle on a stick

**chil-chil** in Nicaragua, a small bell; in Ecuador and Peru, a maraca type shaker

**chinchin** *(Guat.)* maracas

**chinesco** *(Sp.)* bell tree, jingling johnnie

**Chinesische becken** *(Ger.)* Chinese cymbal

**Chinesische blocke** *(Ger.)* Chinese temple blocks

**Chinesische gong** *(Ger.)* tam tam

**Chinesische tom tom** *(Ger.)* Chinese tom tom
**Chinesische zimbel** *(Ger.)* Chinese cymbal
**chocalho** *(Fr., Braz.)* metal tube shaker
**chocalho de metal** *(L. Amer.)* cowbell
**chocalho tubo** *(Fr.)* metal tube shaker
**chocallo** *(L. Amer.)* metal tube shaker
**chocolo** *(L. Amer.)* metal tube shaker
**chucalho** *(Braz.)* metal tube shaker
**chuchas** *(Col.)* maracas
**chucho** *(Col.)* maracas
**cibale antico** *(Sp.)* antique cymbal
**ciembalo** *(Sp.)* cymbal
**cilifono** *(It.)* xylophone
**cimbali antichi** *(It.)* antique cymbal
**cimbalini** *(It.)* antique cymbal
**cimbalo** *(Sp.)* cymbal
**cimbalo antiguo** *(Sp.)* antique cymbal
**cimbalos crapulosos** *(Sp.)* crash cymbals
**cimbalos dedos** *(Sp.)* finger cymbals
**cimbalo suspendido** *(Sp.)* suspended cymbal
**cimbalo suspenso** *(Sp.)* suspended cymbal
**cinellen** *(Ger.)* cymbal
**cinelli** *(It.)* crash cymbals
**cinelli dito** *(It.)* finger cymbals
**clacson** *(It.)* automobile horn, taxi horn
**clagnebois** *(Fr.)* xylophone
**claquebois** *(Fr.)* xylophone
**clavequebois** *(Fr.)* keyboard xylophone
**cliquet** *(Fr.)* slapstick
**cliquette** *(Fr.)* slapstick
**cloche(s) à vache(s)** *(Fr.)* cowbell(s)
**cloche de vache** *(Fr.)* cowbell
**cloche en lame de metal** *(Fr.)* bell plate
**cloches** *(Fr.)* chimes
**cloches éoliennes** *(Fr.)* aeolian bells
**cloches plagues** *(Fr.)* bell plate
**cloches tubulaires** *(Fr.)* chimes
**clochette** *(Fr.)* Buddha temple bell
**clochettes** *(Fr.)* orchestra bells
**clochettes a mains** *(Fr.)* hand bells
**clochettes pour la messe** *(Fr.)* santus bells
**coco** *(S. Amer.)* wood block
**conard** *(Fr.)* duck call
**conga trommel** *(Ger.)* conga drum
**congos** *(Pol.)* congas
**copólogo** *(Sp.)* tuned glasses
**coquilles noix de coco** *(Fr.)* coconut shells

**cor d'auto** *(Fr.)* automobile horn
**coreani** *(It.)* temple blocks
**corno di automobile** *(It.)* automobile horn
**coucou** *(Fr.)* cuckoo call
**coudhoúnia** *(Gr.)* tuned cowbells
**coup de bouchon** *(Fr.)* pop gun
**coup de marteau** *(Fr.)* hammer
**coup de pistolet** *(Fr.)* pistol shot
**coupes de verre** *(Fr.)* tuned glasses
**coutália** *(Gr.)* wooden spoons
**crécelle** *(Fr.)* ratchet
**creole(s)** *(Fr.)* timbales
**crotales** *(Fr., Sp.)* antique cymbals
**crotales antiques** *(Fr.)* antique cymbals
**crotali(o)** *(It.)* antique cymbals
**crotalos** *(Sp.)* antique cymbals
**crystallophone** *(Fr.)* tuned glasses
**cuculo** *(It.)* cuckoo call
**cuerno de auto** *(Sp.)* automobile horn
**cununú** *(Col.)* large Colombian jungle drum
**cymbale(s)** *(Fr.)* cymbal
**cymbale chareston** *(Fr.)* hi-hat
**cymbale charleston à pedale** *(Fr.)* hi-hat
**cymbale Chinoise** *(Fr.)* Chinese cymbal
**cymbale dedos** *(Sp.)* finger cymbals
**cymbale doigte** *(Fr.)* finger cymbals
**cymbale fixée à la grosse caisse** *(Fr.)* cymbal attached to the bass drum
**cymbale libre** *(Fr.)* suspended cymbal
**cymbale sur tiges** *(Fr.)* sizzle cymbal
**cymbale suspendue** *(Fr.)* suspended cymbal
**cymbales á2** *(Fr.)* crash cymbals
**cymbales á l'ordinaire** *(Fr.)* crash cymbals
**cymbales antiques** *(Fr.)* antique cymbals
**cymbales á pedale** *(Fr.)* hi-hat
**cymbales avec platèaux** *(Fr.)* crash cymbals
**cymbales charleston** *(Fr.)* hi-hat
**cymbales digitales** *(Fr.)* finger cymbals
**cymbali antichi** *(It.)* antique cymbals
**cymbels** *(Fr.)* cymbals

# D

**dadoo** *(L. Amer.)* large maraca
**damphu** *(Afr.)* tambourine
**darabukka** *(Ger.)* Arabian hand drum
**darboukka** *(Fr.)* Arabian hand drum
**derbouka** *(Fr.)* Arabian hand drum

**derbuka** *(Ger.)* Arabian hand drum
**derevyánnaya koróbochka** *(Rus.)* wood block
**deux plateaux** *(Fr.)* crash cymbals
**dhol** *(Afr.)* cylindrical wedding drum
**diable des bois** *(Fr.)* pasteboard rattle
**diavolo di bosco** *(It.)* pasteboard rattle
**die einfell tom tom** *(Ger.)* single-headed tom tom
**dobači** *(Ger., It., Fr.)* Japanese temple bell
**donnerblech** *(Ger.)* thunder sheet
**donner-machine** *(Ger.)* thunder sheet
**donnermaschine** *(Ger.)* thunder sheet
**doppelkonustrommel** *(Ger.)* double conical drum
**drévnie tarélki** *(Rus.)* antique cymbals

# E

**echelette** *(Fr.)* xylophone
**l'effetto di pioggia** *(It.)* rain machine
**einfellige grosse trommel** *(Ger.)* gong bass drum
**eisenröhre** *(Ger.)* iron pipe
**ekon** *(L. Amer.)* cowbell
**ekwe** *(Afr.)* slit drum
**elefantenglocke** *(Ger.)* elephant bells
**l'enclume** *(Fr.)* anvil
**enkanika** *(L. Amer.)* square cowbell
**entenquak** *(Ger.)* duck call
**eolifono** *(It.)* wind machine
**eoliophone** *(Fr.)* wind machine
**l'éoliphone** *(Fr.)* wind machine
**eperons** *(Fr.)* spurs
**esquila** *(Sp.)* cowbell

# F

**fanitscharspil** *(Dan.)* jingling johnnie
**fasstrommel(n)** *(Ger.)* barrel drum
**ferraña** *(Sp.)* tambourine without the head
**ferreñas** *(Sp.)* tambourine without the head
**fingerbecken** *(Ger.)* finger cymbals
**fingerzimbeln** *(Ger.)* finger cymbals
**fischi d'uccelli** *(It.)* bird whistle
**fischietto a pallina** *(It.)* police whistle
**fischio** *(It.)* boat or train whistle
**fischio sirena** *(It.)* mouth siren
**flagello** *(It.)* slapstick
**flaschenkorkenknall** *(Ger.)* pop gun
**flaschenspiel** *(Ger.)* tuned bottles

**flauto a culisse** *(It.)* slide whistle
**flessatono** *(It.)* flexatone
**flexaton** *(Ger.)* flexatone
**foglie die rame** *(It.)* metal wind chimes
**foglio di metallo** *(It.)* foil rattle
**fouet** *(Fr.)* slapstick
**frei becken** *(Ger.)* suspended cymbal
**freihängend** *(Ger.)* suspended cymbal
**frusta** *(It.)* slapstick
**furruco** *(Ven.)* large Venezuelan friction drum
**fussbecken** *(Ger.)* hi-hat
**fusta** *(Sp.)* slapstick

# G

**gabelbecken** *(Ger.)* cymbal tongs
**gangarria** *(L. Amer.)* cowbell
**ganza** *(Braz.)* metal tube shaker
**gariglione** *(It.)* church bells
**gebetsqlocke** *(Ger.)* temple bell
**gegenschlagblöcke** *(Ger.)* concussion blocks
**gegenschlagstäbe** *(Ger.)* claves
**gelaute** *(Ger.)* cowbell with clapper
**gewöhnlich mit tellern** *(Ger.)* crash cymbals
**ghungru** *(Ind.)* ankle bells
**Giavanese gong** *(It.)* Java nipple gong
**gigelina** *(It.)* xylophone

**gigelira** *(It.)* xylophone
**gilim gilim** *(Port.)* Brazilian bell tree
**gitterrassel** *(Ger.)* angklung
**gläser** *(Ger.)* glass harmonica
**gläserspiel** *(Ger.)* tuned glasses
**glasharfe** *(Ger.)* glass harp
**glasharmonika** *(Ger.)* glass harmonica
**glaspapier** *(Ger.)* sandpaper
**glasspiel** *(Ger.)* tuned glasses
**glasstabchen** *(Ger.)* glass wind chimes
**glasstabe** *(Ger.)* glass wind chimes
**glasstäbe hängenden** *(Ger.)* glass wind chimes
**glas-windglocken** *(Ger.)* glass wind chimes
**glöckchen** *(Ger.)* chimes
**glocke** *(Ger.)* bell
**glocken** *(Ger.)* chimes
**glockenplatten** *(Ger.)* bell plates
**glockenrad** *(Ger.)* bell wheel

**glockenspiel** *(Ger.)* orchestra bells

**glockenspiel à clavier** *(Fr.)* keyboard glockenspiel

**glockenspiel mit tasten** *(Ger.)* keyboard orchestra bells

**glockenstab** *(Ger.)* bell bar

**glocke tiefe** *(Ger.)* church or steeple bell

**glymbals...** cymbals

**gong à mamelon** *(Fr.)* nipple gong

**gong Giapponese** *(It.)* nipple gong

**gong Giavanese** *(It.)* nipple gong

**gong medio suspeso** *(It.)* medium suspended gong

**gong sospesi** *(It.)* suspended gong

**gonga grande** *(Sp.)* large nipple gong

**gonga pequeño** *(Sp.)* small nipple gong

**gonghi** *(It.)* gong

**gonghi Thailandesi** *(Pol.)* Thailand gong

**gongo** *(Sp.)* gong

**gongstrommel** *(Ger.)* steel drum

**goyom** *(Guat.)* marimba

**gracidio di anitra** *(It.)* duck call

**grage** *(L. Amer.)* guiro type gourd scraper

**gran cassa** *(It.)* bass drum

**gran cassa a una pelle** *(It.)* gong bass drum

**gran cassa catuba** *(It.)* bass drum

**gran tamburo** *(It.)* bass drum

**gran tamburo vecchio** *(It.)* long drum with snares

**grand tambour** *(Fr.)* long drum with snares

**grande cloche** *(Fr.)* church or steeple bell

**gregge** *(It.)* cowbell

**grelots** *(Fr.)* sleighbells

**grelots de vaches** *(Fr.)* cowbell

**griffklapper** *(Ger.)* slapstick

**grijutians** *(Mex.)* rattle

**grosse caisse** *(Fr.)* bass drum

**grosse caisse a pied avec cymbale** *(Fr.)* bass drum pedal with cymbal

**grosse caisse à une seule peau** *(Fr.)* gong bass drum

**grosse caisse avec pedale** *(Fr.)* bass drum with a floor pedal

**gross pauke** *(Ger.)* large timpany

**grosse ruehrtrommel** *(Ger.)* large tenor drum

**grosse ruhrtrommel** *(Ger.)* large tenor drum

**grosse tiefe holztrommel** *(Ger.)* large, low sounding slit drum

**grosse trommel** *(Ger.)* bass drum

**grosses hängendes becken** *(Ger.)* large suspended cymbal

**grosses tam tam** *(Ger.)* large tam tam

**gr. ruhrtrommel** *(Ger.)* large field drum

**guacharaca** *(Col.)* guiro

**guaché** *(Col.)* wooden shaker

**guajey** *(L. Amer.)* large maraca type gourd rattle

**guarará** *(Braz.)* metal tube shaker

**guayo** *(L. Amer.)* guiro type gourd scraper

**guimbarde** *(Fr.)* jaw's (Jew's) harp

**guira** *(L. Amer.)* cabasa

**guirro** *(It.)* guiro

**guitcharo** *(Fr.)* gourd scraper

**guyada** *(Sp.)* vibraslap

# H

**hammerschlag** *(Ger.)* hammer

**handglockenspiel** *(Ger.)* hand bells

**handratsche** *(Ger.)* ratchet

**handtrommel** *(Ger.)* tambourine

**hängebecken** *(Ger.)* suspended cymbal

**hängende bambusrohre** *(Ger.)* suspended bamboo wind chimes

**hangende glasplattchen** *(Ger.)* glass wind chimes

**hängendes becken** *(Ger.)* suspended cymbal

**harmonica de bois** *(Fr.)* xylophone

**harmonica de Franklin** *(Fr.)* glass harmonica

**l'harmonica de verre** *(Fr.)* glass harmonica

**harpe de verre** *(Fr.)* tuned glasses

**heerdenglocken** *(Ger.)* cowbells

**herdenglocken** *(Ger.)* cowbells

**hi-hat becken** *(Ger.)* hi-hat

**hi-hat maschine** *(Ger.)* hi-hat

**hit-hat** *(Pol.)* hi-hat

**hochet** *(Braz.)* maracas

**hochette** *(Fr.)* baby rattle

**holzblock** *(Ger.)* wood block

**holzblöcke** *(Ger.)* wood block

**holzblocktrommel** *(Ger.)* wood block

**holzfass** *(Ger.)* barrel drum

**holzharmonika** *(Ger.)* xylophone

**holzkasten** *(Ger.)* wood block

**holzklapper** *(Ger.)* slapstick

**holzplattentrommel** *(Ger.)* wood plate drum

**holzraspel** *(Ger.)* wooden scraper

**holzstab** *(Ger.)* claves

**holzstabspiel** *(Ger.)* xylophone

**holz tom tom** *(Ger.)* barrel drum

**holz und schlaginstrument** *(Ger.)* xylophone

**holz und strohinstrument** *(Ger.)* xylophone

**holz und strohinstrumente** *(Ger.)* four row xylophone

**holz windglocken** *(Ger.)* bamboo wind chimes

**holzton** *(Ger.)* wood block

**holztrommel** *(Ger.)* wood drum, slit drum

**huada** *(Chile)* maracas

**huehuetl** *(Mex. Ind.)* large ornately covered single headed wooden drum
**hufgetrappel** *(Ger.)* hoofbeats
**hul** *(L. Amer.)* slit drum
**hupe** *(claxon) (Ger.)* klaxon horn
**hyoshige** *(Jap.)* concussion blocks
**hyoshigi** *(Ger., Fr., It.)* concussion blocks

# I

**ieumai** *(Ven.)* maracas
**l'incudine** *(It.)* anvil
**Indianische trommel** *(Ger.)* American Indian drum
**Indianischer trommel** *(Ger.)* American Indian drum
**Indianischo schellen** *(Ger.)* Indian chimes
**Indische schellenband ghungru** *(Ger.)* Indian bell strap
**instrumento d'acciaio** *(It.)* orchestra bells

# J

**Japanische tempelglocken** *(Ger.)* Japanese temple bell
**Javanischer buckelgong** *(Ger.)* nipple gong
**jazzbatterie** *(Ger.)* drum set
**jazzo flûte** *(Fr.)* slide whistle
**jeu à tubes** *(Fr.)* chimes
**jeu de cloche(s)** *(Fr.)* chimes
**jeu de clochettes** *(Fr.)* orchestra bells
**jeu de timbres** *(Fr.)* orchestra bells
**jeux de timbres à clavier** *(Fr.)* orchestra bells, keyboard glockenspiel
**jicara de agua** *(Mex. Ind.)* water gourd
**joca** *(L. Amer.)* large single headed conga type drum
**juca** *(L. Amer.)* friction drum
**juco** *(L. Amer.)* lion's roar
**juego de campanas** *(Sp.)* chimes
**juego de timbres** *(Sp.)* orchestra bells
**juque** *(L. Amer.)* lion's roar

# K

**kamesa** *(S. Amer.)* shaker
**kameso** *(Afr.)* shaker
**kanone** *(Ger.)* cannon shot
**kartal** *(Afr.)* cymbals
**karutaná** *(Braz.)* stamping tube
**kastagnetten** *(Ger.)* castanets
**kastan'ety** *(Rus.)* castanets
**kastaniety** *(Pol.)* castanets
**kegeltrommel** *(Ger.)* conical drum

**keiselsteine** *(Ger.)* stones
**kelchglaser** *(Ger.)* cupglasses
**kempul** *(Or.)* gong
**kesselgong** *(Ger.)* kettle gong
**kesselpauke** *(Ger.)* timpany
**kesselpauken** *(Ger.)* timpany
**kesseltrommel** *(Ger.)* timpany
**ketten** *(Ger.)* iron chains
**kettenrassel** *(Ger.)* iron chains
**khanjeri** *(Afr.)* tambourine
**kinderspeilzeugtrommel** *(Ger.)* toy drum
**kirchenglocken** *(Ger.)* church bells
**kiyada** *(L. Amer.)* jawbone
**klapper** *(Ger.)* slapstick
**klappholz** *(Ger.)* slapstick
**kláves** *(Rus.)* claves
**klaviaturglockenspiel** *(Ger.)* keyboard orchestra bells
**klaviaturxylophon** *(Ger.)* keyboard xylophone
**klaxon** *(Ger., Fr.)* hand cranked auto horn
**klaxon à manivelle** *(Fr.)* mechanized klaxon
**kleine trommel** *(Ger.)* snare drum
**kleine trommeln** *(Ger.)* snare drum
**kleines hängendes becken** *(Ger.)* small suspended cymbal
**kleines tam tam** *(Ger.)* small tam tam
**klingsteine** *(Ger.)* stones
**knarre** *(Ger.)* ratchet
**knochenklapper** *(Ger.)* bones
**knut** *(Rus.)* slapstick
**ko-daiko** *(Jap.)* small cylindrical drum with two heads
**kokiriko** *(Jap.)* bin zasara
**kokosnuss schalen** *(Ger.)* coconut shells
**kolokól'chiki** *(Rus.)* orchestra bells
**konustrommel(n)** *(Ger.)* conical drum
**konzert trommel** *(Ger.)* snare drum
**krotalen** *(Ger.)* antique cymbals
**krotalon** *(Ger.)* antique cymbals
**krug** *(Ger.)* jug
**krystallophon** *(Ger.)* tuned glasses
**ksilofón** *(Rus.)* xylophone
**kuba-pauken** *(Ger.)* timbales
**kuckuck instrument** *(Ger.)* cuckoo call
**kuckucksruf** *(Ger.)* cuckoo call
**kuhglocke(n)** *(Ger.)* cowbell
**kuhglocken** *(Ger.)* cowbell
**kuhglocke(n) ohne klöppel** *(Ger.)* cowbell without clapper
**kuhschelle** *(Ger.)* cowbell
**kurbis** *(Ger.)* gourd
**kürbisraspel** *(Ger.)* gourd rattle

# L

**lame musicale** *(Fr.)* musical saw
**lamina metalica** *(Sp.)* thunder sheet
**landsknechtstrommel** *(Ger.)* military snare drum
**lastra dal tuono** *(It.)* thunder sheet
**lastra del tuono** *(It.)* thunder sheet
**lastra di latta** *(It.)* thunder sheet
**lastra di metallo** *(It.)* fighter's bell
**lastra di sasso** *(It.)* stone disks
**lateinamerikanischen** *(Ger.)* timbales
**la tigo** *(Sp.)* slapstick
**leere flaschen** *(Ger.)* empty bottles
**legnetti** *(It.)* claves
**legni di rumba** *(It.)* claves
**legno** *(It.)* wood block
**lero lero** *(It.)* scraper
**libres cymbales** *(Fr.)* suspended cymbals
**litávry** *(Rus.)* timpany
**lithophon** *(Ger.)* lithophone
**litofono** *(Ger.)* lithophone
**lochsirene** *(Ger.)* siren
**lotosflöte** *(Ger.)* slide whistle
**lowengebrull** *(Ger.)* string drum, lion's roar
**lyra-glockenspiel** *(Ger.)* bell lyra

# M

**macchina a venti** *(It.)* wind machine
**macchina dal vento** *(It.)* wind machine
**macchina del vento** *(It.)* wind machine
**macchina di tuono(i)** *(It.)* thunder sheet
**machine à tonnerre** *(Fr.)* thunder sheet
**machine à vent** *(Fr.)* wind machine
**machine à venti** *(It.)* wind machine
**macillo** *(Sp.)* hammer
**maguey** *(L. Amer.)* slit drum
**mályi barabán** *(Rus.)* snare drum
**mamelon** *(Fr.)* nipple gong
**manguara** *(L. Amer.)* slit drum
**manguare'** *(Col.)* tuned log
**maquina de trueno** *(Sp.)* thunder sheet
**maquina de viento** *(Sp.)* wind machine
**maraca de métal** *(Fr.)* metal rattle
**maraca di metallo** *(It.)* metal rattle
**marache** *(It.)* maracas
**marákas** *(Rus.)* maracas

**mardala** *(Ind.)* mirdangam

**marimbafono** *(It.)* marimba

**marimbaphon** *(Ger.)* marimba

**marimbaphone** *(Fr.)* marimba

**marteau** *(Fr.)* hammer

**marteaux** *(Fr.)* hammers

**martello** *(It.)* hammer

**martelo** *(Port.)* hammer

**maruga** *(Cuban)* maracas

**mascella d'asino** *(It.)* vibraslap

**massá** *(Gr.)* cymbal tongs

**matraca** *(Sp.)* ratchet

**matraco** *(Sp.)* large cowbell

**maultrommel** *(Ger.)* jaw's (Jew's) harp

**maychil**   in Nicaragua, a small bell; in Ecuador and Peru, a maraca type shaker

**mbira** *(Afr.)* marimbula

**megalo´** *(Braz.)* bull roarer or thunder stick

**messklingeln** *(Ger.)* sanctus bells

**metallblock** *(Ger.)* anvil

**metallfolie** *(Ger.)* thunder sheet

**metallgefässrassel** *(Ger.)* metal rattle

**metallkastagnetten** *(Ger.)* metal castanets

**metallkasten** *(Ger.)* metal block

**metallofono** *(It.)* metallophone

**metallophon** *(Ger.)* metallophone

**metallplatte** *(Ger.)* fighter's bell

**metall raspel** *(Ger.)* metal scraper

**metall-windglocken** *(Ger.)* metal wind chimes

**metlá** *(Rus.)* switch

**militärtrommel** *(Ger.)* military drum

**mirlitons** *(Ger.)* kazoos

**mit teller** *(Ger.)* crash cymbals

**mit tellern** *(Ger.)* crash cymbals

**mula** *(L. Amer.)* single headed conga type drum

**muschel windglocken** *(Ger.)* shell wind chimes

# N

**nacchera cilindrica** *(It.)* tubular wood block

**nacchere** *(It.)* castanets

**nachtigall** *(Ger.)* nightingale

**nachtigallenschlag** *(Ger.)* nightingale

**nagara** *(Ind.)* large timpany

**nakovál'nya** *(Rus.)* anvil

**naruco** *(It.)* wooden wind chimes

**naruko** *(Jap.)* bamboo wind chimes

**nebelhorn** *(Ger.)* fog horn

**nietenbecken** *(Ger.)* sizzle cymbal
**ni-shoko** *(Jap.)* small gong
**noce di cocco** *(It.)* coconut shells
**noix de coco** *(Fr.)* maracas

# O

**o-daiko** *(Jap.)* Chinese tom tom
**okwa** *(Afr.)* log drum
**organo di legna** *(It.)* xylophone
**ouay** *(Braz.)* metal tube shaker

# P

**paarweise becken** *(Ger.)* crash cymbals
**pailla** *(Sp.)* timbale shell
**paio di piatti** *(It.)* pair of cymbals
**paire de cymbales** *(Fr.)* pair of crash cymbals
**palo bufonesco** *(Sp.)* slapstick
**palo zumbador** *(Sp.)* bull roarer
**pandeiro** *(Port.)* tambourine
**pandereta** *(Sp.)* tambourine
**pandereta brasiliano** *(It.)* pandereta brasileño
**pandéréta brésilienne** *(Fr.)* pandereta brasileño
**pandero** *(Sp.)* tambourine
**pandero grande** *(S. Amer.)* tambourine without jingles
**pandero pequeno** *(S. Amer.)* tambourine with jingles
**pandorella** *(Sp.)* tambourine without a head
**panhuehuetl** *(Mex. Ind.)* a medium size ornately covered single headed wooden drum
**papel de lija** *(Sp.)* sandpaper blocks
**papier de verre** *(Fr.)* sandpaper blocks
**paradetrommel** *(Ger.)* parade drum
**pas de cheval** *(Fr.)* hoofbeats
**patouilles** *(Fr.)* xylophone
**pauke** *(Ger.)* timpany
**pauken** *(Ger.)* timpany
**pavillon Chinois** *(Fr.)* jingling johnnie
**pedalpauke** *(Ger.)* timpany with pedals
**peitsche** *(Ger.)* slapstick
**pietschenknall** *(Ger.)* slapstick
**percussione** *(It.)* percussion
**perkusie** *(Pol.)* percussion
**perkuste** *(Pol.)* percussion
**petit tambour** *(Fr.)* piccolo snare drum
**petit tambour san timbre** *(Fr.)* small snare drum without snares
**petite caisse claire** *(Fr.)* piccolo snare drum
**petite tambour** *(Fr.)* piccolo snare drum
**petite timbale** *(Fr.)* piccolo timpany

**phonolithes** *(Fr.)* stones
**piano Africano** *(Sp.)* marimba
**piano de cuia** *(Braz.)* a double rattle on a stick
**piatti** *(It.)* cymbals
**piatti a2** *(It.)* crash cymbals
**piatti a due** *(It.)* crash cymbals
**piatti antichi** *(It.)* antique cymbals
**piatti a pedale** *(It.)* hi-hat
**piatti charleston** *(It.)* hi-hat
**piatti Cinesi** *(It.)* Chinese cymbal
**piatti sospesi** *(It.)* suspended cymbal
**piatto** *(It.)* suspended cymbal
**piatto Chinoso** *(It.)* Chinese cymbal
**piatto chiodat** *(It.)* sizzle cymbal
**piatto Cinese** *(It.)* Chinese cymbal
**piatto fissato** *(It.)* suspended cymbal
**piatto piccado sospesi** *(It.)* small suspended cymbal
**piatto sospeso** *(It.)* suspended cymbal
**piatto uniti ala gran cassa** *(It.)* bass drum with cymbal attached
**piccolo cassa** *(It.)* piccolo snare drum
**piccolo timpani orientali** *(It.)* piccolo timpany
**pierres** *(Fr.)* stones
**pietra sonora** *(It.)* stones
**pikkolotrommel** *(Ger.)* piccolo snare drum
**pistolenschoss** *(Ger.)* pistol shot
**pistolenschuss** *(Ger.)* pistol shot
**pistolettata** *(It.)* pistol shot
**piuta** *(Braz.)* friction drum
**planchette ronflante** *(Fr.)* bull roarer
**plaque de metál** *(Fr.)* fighter's bell
**plaque de tonnerre** *(Fr.)* thunder sheet
**plaques epaisses** *(Fr.)* thick plates
**plateaux** *(Fr.)* crash cymbals
**platillos** *(Sp.)* crash cymbals
**platos** *(Sp.)* crash cymbals
**plattenglocke(n)** *(Ger.)* bell plate
**podvéshennaya tarelka** *(Rus.)* suspended cymbal
**pogremúshka** *(Rus.)* rattle
**polizeiflote** *(Ger.)* police whistle
**prato de bronze** *(S. Amer.)* cymbal
**prisme de pluie** *(Fr.)* rain machine
**provansal'skii barabán** *(Rus.)* tabor
**provencal tambourin** *(Fr.)* tabor
**provenzale** *(It.)* tabor
**provenzalische trommel** *(Ger.)* military snare drum without the snares
**psalterium ligneum** *(Lat.)* xylophone

puita *(S. Amer.)* cuica
pulgaretes *(Sp.)* castanets
pulgarillas *(Sp.)* castanets

# Q

quaisi canone *(It.)* cannon shot
quica *(S. Amer.)* friction drum
quijada *(S. Amer.)* jawbone (of an ass)
quijada del burro *(Cuban)* jawbone (of an ass) ornamented with bells
quyada *(Fr.)* jawbone (of an ass)

# R

rachet...ratchet
racle *(Fr.)* scraper
racleur *(Fr.)* scraper
raganella *(It.)* ratchet
rahmenrassel *(Ger.)* frame rattle
rahmentrommel *(Ger.)* frame drum
râpe *(Fr.)* guiro
rape á fromage *(Fr.)* a cheese grater
râpe de bois *(Fr.)* wooden scraper
râpe de métal *(Fr.)* metal scraper
râpe quiro *(Fr.)* guiro
raspadero *(Sp.)* guiro
raspa di metallo *(It.)* metal scraper
raspador *(Sp.)* any type of scraper
raspe *(It.)* scraper
raspel *(Ger.)* scraper
rassel *(Ger.)* rattle
rasseln *(Ger.)* maracas
rasseltrommel *(Ger.)* rattle drum
ratsche *(Ger.)* ratchet
rebube *(Fr.)* jaw's (Jew's) harp
reco-reco *(Ger., Fr., It.)* bamboo scraper
redeblante *(Sp.)* tenor drum
redoblante *(Sp.)* tenor drum
régale de bois *(Fr.)* xylophone
régale de percussion *(Fr.)* xylophone
regenmaschine *(Ger.)* rain machine
regenprisma *(Ger.)* rain machine
reibtrommel *(Ger.)* friction drum, lion's roar
reihenklapper *(Ger.)* bin zasara
resonanzkastenxylophon *(Ger.)* trough xylophone
reso-reso *(It.)* wooden scraper
revolver *(Ger., Fr.)* pistol shot
rhombe *(Fr.)* bull roarer

**ribeba** *(It.)* jaw's (Jew's) harp

**richiamo de uccelli** *(It.)* bird call

**richiamo per uccelli** *(It.)* bird whistle

**rivoltella** *(It.)* pistol shot

**röhrenglocke(n)** *(Ger.)* chimes

**röhrenglockenspiel** *(Ger.)* chimes

**röhrenholztrommel** *(Ger.)* tubular wood blocks

**röhrentrommel** *(Ger.)* cylindrical drum

**rolliertrommel** *(Ger.)* tenor drum

**rollschellen** *(Ger.)* sleighbells

**rolltrommel** *(Ger.)* tenor drum

**rombo sonore** *(It.)* bull roarer

**rommelpot** *(Ger.)* friction drum

**roncador** *(L. Amer.)* friction drum

**roto tom accordé manuellement** *(Fr.)* hand tuned roto tom

**roto tom afinado a mano** *(Sp.)* hand tuned roto tom

**roto tom afinado a pedale (y también a mano)** *(Sp.)* pedal tuned, as well as, hand tuned roto tom

**roto tom à pédale (peut aussi être accordé manuellement)** *(Fr.)* pedal tuned, as well as, hand tuned roto tom

**roto tom hangestimmt** *(Ger.)* hand tuned roto tom

**roto tom pedalgestimmt und handgestimmt** *(Ger.)* pedal tuned, as well as, hand tuned roto tom

**roue à clochettes** *(Fr.)* bell wheel

**rove de la loterie** *(Fr.)* lottery wheel. A small ratchet is usually substituted.

**rugghio di leone** *(It.)* lion's roar

**ruggio di leone** *(It.)* lion's roar

**ruggito** *(It.)* lion's roar

**ruggito del leone** *(It.)* lion's roar

**rugir de leon** *(Sp.)* lion's roar

**rugissement de lion** *(Fr.)* lion's roar

**rüghrtrommel** *(Ger.)* field drum

**rührtrommel hoch** *(Ger.)* a high pitch field drum

**rührtrommel ohne saiten** *(Ger.)* tenor drum

**rührtrommel tief** *(Ger.)* long drum with snares

**rumbabirne** *(Ger.)* maracas

**rumbaholz** *(Ger.)* claves

**rumbakugeln** *(Ger.)* maracas

**rute** *(Ger.)* switch

**ruthe** *(Ger.)* switch

# S

**sablier** *(Fr.)* sandbox

**saccapá** *(Andean)* an Andean jingle rattle

**säge** *(Ger.)* musical saw

**sakefass** *(Ger.)* sake barrel

**sandblöcke** *(Ger.)* sandpaper blocks

**sandbüchse** *(Ger.)* maracas

**sandpapier** *(Ger.)* sandpaper blocks

**sandpapierblocke** *(Fr., Ger.)* sandpaper blocks

**sandrassel** *(Ger.)* sandbox

**sanduhrtrommel** *(Ger.)* hourglass drum

**sapo Cubana** *(Ger., Fr., It.)* bamboo guiro

**sarténes** *(S. Amer.)* frying pans

**sassi** *(It.)* stones

**scacciapensieri** *(It.)* jaw's (Jew's) harp

**scampanellio da gregge** *(It.)* cowbells

**schalenglöckchen** *(Ger.)* Buddha temple bell

**schallbecken** *(Ger.)* cymbals

**schelle** *(Ger.)* jingles

**schellen** *(Ger.)* sleighbells

**schellenbaum** *(Ger.)* jingling johnnie

**schellenbäume** *(Ger.)* jingling johnnie

**schellenbündel** *(Ger.)* sleighbells bunched together

**schellen rassel** *(Ger.)* tambourine without a head

**schellenreif** *(Ger.)* tambourine without a head

**schellentamburin** *(Ger.)* tambourine

**schellentrommel** *(Ger.)* tambourine

**schiffsglocke** *(Ger.)* ship's bell

**schirrholz** *(Ger.)* bull roarer

**schlagbrett** *(Ger.)* wooden board

**schlagrassel** *(Ger.)* vibraslap

**schlagstabe** *(Ger.)* claves

**schlagzeug** *(Ger.)* percussion, drum set, drums

**schlittelrohr** *(Ger.)* metal tube shaker

**schlitten-schellen** *(Ger.)* tuned sleighbells

**schlitztrommel** *(Ger.)* slit drum

**schmirgelblock** *(Ger.)* sandpaper block

**schnarre** *(Ger.)* ratchet

**schotenrassel** *(Ger.)* pod shakers

**schnurrassel** *(Ger.)* strung rattle

**schotenrassel** *(Ger.)* pod shakes

**schraper** *(Ger.)* scraper

**schüttelrohr** *(Ger.)* metal tube shaker

**schwirrholz** *(Ger.)* bull roarer

**scie musicale(a)** *(Fr.)* musical saw

**sega** *(It.)* musical saw

**sega cantante** *(It.)* musical saw

**sehrhoch** *(Ger.)* snare drum

**sguilla** *(It.)* cowbell

**shekeres** *(Afr.)* afuche

**shellentrommel** *(Ger.)* tambourine

**shoko** *(Jap.)* gong

**sifflet à coulisse** *(Fr.)* slide whistle

**sifflet à roulette** *(Fr.)* police whistle

**sifflet d'oiseau** *(Fr.)* bird whistle

**sifflet imeté du rossignol** *(Fr.)* nightingale

**sifflet signal** *(Fr.)* signal whistle

**sifflet sirène** *(Fr.)* mouth siren

**signalpfeife** *(Ger.)* signal whistle

**silofone** *(It.)* xylophone

**silfono** *(It.)* xylophone

**silofono a tastiera** *(It.)* keyboard xylophone

**silofono basso** *(It.)* bass xylophone

**silomarimba** *(It.)* xylomarimba

**silophono** *(It.)* xylophone

**simandron...**a wooden board

**sineta** *(S. Amer.)* small bell

**singende säge** *(Ger.)* musical saw

**sirena** *(It., Sp.)* siren

**sirena bass** *(It.)* fog horn

**sirena a fiato** *(It.)* mouth siren

**sirena a mano** *(It.)* siren

**sirena da battelo** *(It.)* warning siren

**sirene** *(Ger., Fr.)* police siren

**sirène a bouche** *(Fr.)* mouth siren

**sirene aigue** *(Fr.)* police siren

**sirène grave** *(Fr.)* low siren

**sirenenpfeife** *(Ger.)* mouth siren

**sistra** *(It.)* sistrum

**sistre** *(Fr.)* sistrum

**sistro** *(It.)* triangle

**soalha** *(Port.)* jingles

**sonagli** *(It.)* sleighbells

**sonagli a mano** *(It.)* hand bells

**songali Inciana** *(It.)* Indian chimes

**sonagliera** *(It.)* sleighbells

**sonaglio** *(It.)* Buddha temple bell

**sonaja** *(Mex. Ind.)* maracas

**sonajas** *(Sp.)* sleighbells

**sonajero** *(Sp.)* rattle

**soneria di campane** *(It.)* chimes

**sonnailles** *(Fr.)* cowbell

**sonailles de troupeau** *(Fr.)* Alpine herd bells

**sonailles sur bâton** *(Fr.)* stick rattle

**sonnette de table** *(Fr.)* dinner bell

**speroni** *(It.)* spurs

**spielsäge** *(Ger.)* musical saw

**sporen** *(Ger.)* spurs

**sproni** *(It.)* spurs

**stabglockenspiel** *(Ger.)* orchestra bells

**stabpandereta** *(Ger.)* jingle stick

**stabrassel** *(Ger.)* stick rattle

**stabspiel** *(Ger.)* metallophone

**stahllöffel** *(Ger.)* steel spoons

**stahlspel** *(Ger.)* orchestra bells

**stahltrommel** *(Ger.)* steel drum

**stampfrohr** *(Ger.)* stamping tube

**stampftrommel** *(Ger.)* stamping tube

**standglocke** *(Ger.)* temple bell

**stappare la bottiglia** *(It.)* pop gun

**steilkastagnetten** *(Ger.)* finger cymbals

**steinharmonika** *(Ger.)* lithophone

**steinplatten** *(Ger.)* lithophone

**steinspiel** *(Ger.)* lithophone

**stempelflöte** *(Ger.)* slide whistle

**sticcada** *(It.)* xylophone

**sticcado pastorale** *(It.)* keyboard orchestra bells

**sticcato** *(It.)* xylophone

**strohfidel** *(Ger.)* straw xylophone

**strohfiedel** *(Ger.)* straw xylophone

**strosstrommel** *(Ger.)* stamping tube

**sturmglocke** *(Ger.)* storm bell

**suono di bottiglia** *(It.)* tuned bottles

**suono di osso** *(It.)* bones

# T

**taballi** *(It.)* timpany

**tabella** *(It.)* slapstick

**tabla trommein** *(Ger.)* tablas

**table de bois** *(Fr.)* wooden board

**tablette** *(Fr.)* bones

**tabor provencale** *(Fr.)* tabor

**taierze** *(Pol.)* cymbal

**taiko** *(Jap.)* barrel drum

**taletta** *(It.)* bones

**tamb di legno-pelle** *(It.)* wooden tom tom

**tambor** *(L. Amer.)* snare drum

**tambor de fricción** *(Sp.)* friction drum

**tambor de tronco hendido** *(Sp.)* slit drum

**tambor Indio...**Indian drum

**tambor militar** *(Sp.)* snare drum

**tambora** *(Sp.)* bass drum

**tamboreto** *(Sp.)* piccolo snare drum

**tamboril** *(Sp.)* tabor

**tamborilete** *(Sp.)* tamborine

**tamborim** *(Port.)* small one headed drum

**tamborino** *(It.)* tambourine

**tamboron** *(Sp.)* bass drum

**tambour** *(Fr.)* snare drum

**tambour à corde(s)** *(Fr.)* string drum, lion's roar

**tambour à fente** *(Fr.)* slit drum

**tambour à friction** *(Fr.)* friction drum

**tambour Africano** *(S. Amer.)* tambourine without jingles

**tambour Arabe** *(Fr.)* Arabian hand drum

**tambour avec timbre** *(Fr.)* snare drum with snares

**tambour basque** *(Ger.)* tambourine

**tambour con cuerdes** *(Sp.)* lion's roar

**tambour d'acier** *(Fr.)* steel drum

**tambour d'eau** *(Fr.)* water gourd

**tambour d'empire** *(Fr.)* parade drum

**tambour de basque** *(Fr.)* tambourine

**tambour de bois** *(Fr.)* slit drum

**tambour de bois Africain** *(Fr.)* slit drum

**tambour de bronze** *(Fr.)* kettle gong

**tambour de provence** *(Fr.)* tabor

**tambour en cône** *(Fr.)* conical drum

**tambour en cylindre** *(Fr.)* cylindrical drum

**tambour en double cône** *(Fr.)* double conical drum

**tambour en goblet** *(Fr.)* goblet drum

**tambour en peau de bois** *(Fr.)* wood plate drum

**tambour en sablier** *(Fr.)* hourglass drum

**tambour en tonneau** *(Fr.)* barrel drum

**tambour hochet** *(Fr.)* rattle drum

**tambour Indien Américain** *(Fr.)* American Indian drum

**tambour militaire** *(Fr.)* military snare drum

**tambour militaire sans timbre** *(Fr.)* military drum without snares

**tambour petite** *(Fr.)* piccolo snare drum

**tambour provencale** *(Fr.)* tenor drum

**tambour provinsal** *(Fr.)* tabor

**tambour roulante sans cordes** *(Fr.)* tenor drum without snares

**tambour roulante sans timbre** *(Fr.)* tenor drum without snares

**tambour sur cadre** *(Fr.)* frame drum

**tambourin** *(Ger., Fr.)* tenor drum

**tambourin à main** *(Fr.)* hand drum

**tambourin de campagne** *(S. Amer.)* tambourine

**tambourin de provence** *(Fr.)* tabor

**tambourin provecal** *(Fr.)* tabor

**tambourine de samba** *(S. Amer.)* tambourine with jingles

**tambourino** *(It.)* tambourine

**tambours de bois** *(Fr.)* African tree drum

**tambours de frein** *(Fr.)* brake drum

**tamburello** *(It.)* tambourine

**tamburello basco** *(It.)* tambourine

**tamburi** *(Ger., It.)* timpany

**tamburi baschi** *(It.)* tambourine
**tamburi militari senza corde** *(It.)* military snare drum without snares
**tamburi senza corda** *(It.)* snare drum without snares
**tamburin** *(Ger., Rus.)* tambourine
**tamburino** *(It.)* snare drum or tambourine
**tamburino basco** *(It.)* tambourine
**tamburin ohne schellen** *(Ger.)* tambourine without jingles
**tamburino senza cimbali** *(It.)* frame drum

**tamburo** *(It.)* drum
**tamburo acuto** *(Sp., It.)* piccolo snare drum
**tamburo alto** *(It.)* snare drum
**tamburo Arabo** *(It.)* Arabian hand drum
**tamburo basco** *(It.)* tambourine
**tamburo basso** *(It.)* long drum with snares
**tamburo chiara** *(It.)* snare drum
**tamburo con corda** *(It.)* snare drum with snares
**tamburo con corde** *(It.)* snare drum with snares
**tamburo con surino** *(It.)* muted snare drum
**tamburo d'acciaio** *(It.)* steel drum
**tamburo di basilea** *(It.)* parade drum
**tamburo di freno** *(It.)* brake drum
**tamburo di frizione** *(It.)* friction drum
**tamburo di latta** *(It.)* steel drum
**tamburo di legno** *(It.)* log drum
**tamburo di legno a fessura** *(It.)* slit drum
**tamburo di legno Africano** *(It.)* log drum
**tamburo di legno pelle** *(It.)* wood plate drum
**tamburo grande** *(It.)* bass drum
**tamburo grande con corda** *(It.)* a large snare drum with snares
**tamburo grosso** *(It.)* bass drum
**tamburo Indiano d'America** *(It.)* American Indian drum
**tamburo militare** *(It.)* military snare drum
**tamburo orientale** *(It.)* Chinese drum
**tamburo piccolo** *(It.)* piccolo snare drum
**tamburo provenzale** *(It.)* military drum without snares
**tamburo rullante** *(It.)* tenor drum
**tamburo rullante con corde** *(It.)* field drum with snares
**tamburo rullante senza corde** *(It.)* tenor drum without snares
**tamburo senza corda** *(It.)* snare drum without snares
**tamburo sordo** *(S. Amer.)* a muted snare drum or one without snares
**tamburo surdo** *(Port.)* a drum without snares
**tamburone** *(It.)* bass drum
**tam tam grave** *(It.)* a low or deep sounding tam tam
**tam tam tief** *(Ger.)* a low sounding tam tam
**tantã** *(L. Amer.)* gong
**tan tan** *(Sp.)* tom tom
**taquará** *(Braz.)* stamping tube

**tarélki** *(Rus.)* cymbals

**tarol** *(Fr.)* piccolo snare drum

**tarola** *(Sp.)* Mexican timbales

**tarole** *(Fr.)* piccolo snare drum

**tarole Grégoire** *(Fr.)* piccolo snare drum

**tarolle** *(Fr.)* piccolo snare drum

**tavola da lavare** *(It.)* washboard

**tavola di legno** *(It.)* wooden board

**tavoletta** *(It.)* horses hooves

**tavolette** *(It.)* horses hooves

**tela** *(S. Amer.)* buzz marimba

**tellern** *(Ger.)* crash cymbals

**tempelblock(e)** *(Ger.)* temple blocks

**tempelbloki** *(Pol.)* temple blocks

**tempelglocke** *(Ger.)* Japanese temple bells

**temple bloc** *(Fr.)* temple blocks

**templeblöcke** *(Ger.)* temple blocks

**ténabari** *(Mex. Ind.)* a butterfly cocoon rattle made up of hundreds of cocoons

**tenortrommel** *(Ger.)* tenor drum

**teponahuaste** *(L. Amer.)* slit drum

**teponaxtle** *(Mex.)* tuned log

**teponaztli** *(Mex.)* tuned log

**teschio Cinese** *(It.)* Chinese wood blocks

**tetzilacatl** *(Mex.)* gong

**thambatti** *(Ind.)* tambourine

**Tibetanische gebetsteine** *(Ger.)* Tibetan prayer stones

**tichglocke** *(Ger.)* dinner bell

**tiefe glocke** *(Ger.)* Lit. a large bell. A chime or church bell can be substituted.

**tiefe glocken von unbestimmtem klang** *(Ger.)* low bells of indefinite pitch.

**tiefes glockengleläute** *(Ger.)* chimes

**timbal** *(Sp.)* timpany

**timbalão** *(L. Amer)* tenor drum

**timbale(s)** *(Fr., Ger.)* timpany - If it's a German piece, the term refers to timbales.

**timbales chromatiques** *(Fr.)* timpany without shells...Similar to today's roto toms.

**timbales Cubaines** *(Fr.)* timbales

**timbales Cubani** *(It.)* timbales

**timbales Latino-Americani** *(It.)* timbales

**timbales orientale** *(Fr.)* a pair of non pitched, small kettle shaped drums, with thong tensioning

**timb à levier** *(Fr.)* pedal timpany

**timballes** *(Fr.)* timpany

**timballi** *(It.)* timpany

**timballo** *(It.)* timpany

**timbals** *(Sp.)* timpany

**timbrel** *(Sp.)* tambourine

**timbres** *(Fr.)* When dealing with a snare drum, the term means snares. If not, the term means jingles. *Also, see next definition.*

**timbres** *(Sp.)* orchestra bells

**timpanetti** *(It.)* timbales

**timpanetto** *(It.)* timbales

**timpani** *(It.)* timpany

**timpani orientali** *(It.)* a pair of non pitched, small kettle shaped drums, with thong tensioning

**timpano** *(It.)* one timpany

**timpano piccolo** *(It.)* piccolo timpany

**timpano senza pedale** *(It.)* timpany without a pedal

**timpanon** *(Ger.)* tabor

**timplipito** *(Rus.)* a pair of non pitched, small kettle shaped drums, with thong tensioning

**tischglocke** *(Ger.)* dinner bell

**Tlapanhuehuetl** *(Mex. Ind.)* a large ornately covered single headed wooden drum

**toboinha sonante** *(Braz.)* thunder stick

**tocsin** *(Fr.)* alarm bell

**tôle** *(Fr.)* thunder sheet

**tôle pour imiter le tonnerre** *(Fr.)* thunder sheet

**toms à une peau** *(Fr.)* single headed tom tom

**tom tom aigu** *(Fr.)* small tom tom

**tom tom à una pelle** *(It.)* single headed tom tom

**tom tom Chinois** *(Fr.)* Chinese tom tom

**tom tom Cinese** *(It.)* Chinese tom tom

**tom tom grave** *(Fr.)* large tom tom

**tom tom spiel** *(Ger.)* roto toms

**tom tomy** *(Pol.)* tom toms

**tonnant** *(Fr.)* bass drum

**tonnerre à poignée** *(Fr.)* thunder sheet

**tornki** *(Ger.)* belled wooden spoons

**trepei** *(Fr.)* triangle

**treppiede** *(It.)* triangle

**treschotka** *(Rus.)* ratchet

**treugol'nik** *(Rus.)* triangle

**triangel** *(Ger.)* triangle

**triangeln** *(Ger.)* triangle

**triangoli** *(It.)* triangle

**triangolo** *(It.)* triangle

**triangulo** *(Sp.)* triangle

**triangulum** *(Lat.)* triangle

**trigono** *(Gr.)* triangle

**trillerpfeife** *(Ger.)* police whistle

**Trinidad gongtrommel** *(Ger.)* steel drum

**trinquete** *(Sp.)* ratchet

**triphon** *(Ger.)* xylophone

**trogxylophon** *(Ger.)* trough xylophone

**trommel** *(Ger.)* drum
**trompe d'auto** *(Fr.)* taxi horn
**trompe de brume** *(Fr.)* fog horn
**troncs d'arbres** *(Fr.)* log drum
**trúbchatye kolokolá** *(Rus.)* chimes
**tryphone** *(Fr.)* xylophone
**tschinellen** *(Ger.)* cymbals
**tsépi** *(Rus.)* iron chains
**tsilindricheskii barabán** *(Rus.)* tenor drum
**tubalcain...**keyboard xylophone
**tubaphon** *(Ger.)* tubaphone
**tubes, jue de** *(Fr.)* chimes
**tubes de bambou** *(Fr.)* bamboo wind chime(s)
**tube(s) de cloche(s)** *(Fr.)* chimes

**tubi di bambú** *(It.)* bamboo chimes
**tubo** *(It.)* metal tube shaker
**tubo di ferro** *(It.)* iron pipe
**tubofono** *(It.)* tubaphone
**tubolari** *(It.)* chimes
**tubo sonoro** *(It.)* shaker
**tubuscampanophon** *(Ger.)* tubaphone
**tubuscampanophone** *(Ger.)* tubaphone
**tumba** *(Sp., It.)* conga drum
**tumbadora** *(Sp.)* large conga drum
**tun** *(C.A.)* tuned log
**tunoul** *(Mayan)* tuned log
**tunzu** *(L. Amer.)* slit drum
**tuoni** *(It.)* thunder sheet
**tuono a pugno** *(It.)* thunder sheet
**turá-maracá** *(Braz.)* a stamping tube with a maraca tied to it
**turkischen becken** *(Ger.)* crash cymbals
**turmglockenspiel** *(Ger.)* chimes
**tu-ti** *(Saint. Dom.)* castanets
**tuyau de fer** *(Fr.)* iron pipe
**tympali** *(Ger.)* timpany
**tympana** *(L. Amer.)* timpany
**tympani** *(L. Amer.)* timpany
**tympano** *(It.)* timpany
**tympelles** *(Ger.)* timpany
**tzicahuaztli** *(Mex. Ind.)* guiro

# U

**uccelli** *(It.)* bird whistle
**udárnye instruménty** *(Rus.)* percussion
**l'usignuolo** *(It.)* nightingale

# V

**verga** *(It.)* switch
**verge(s)** *(Fr.)* switch(s)
**verghe** *(It.)* switch
**verres choqués** *(Fr.)* glass harmonica
**verrillon** *(Fr.)* tuned glasses
**vetrata** *(It.)* sandpaper blocks
**vibrafón** *(Rus.)* vibraphone
**vibrafoni** *(It.)* vibraphone
**vibrafono** *(It.)* vibraphone
**vibraphon** *(Ger., Rus.)* vibraphone
**viehschelle(n)** *(Ger.)* cowbell
**vieschelle** *(Ger.)* cowbell
**voénnyi barabán** *(Rus.)* military snare drum
**vogel-lockruf** *(Ger.)* bird call
**vogelpfeife** *(Ger.)* bird whistle

# W

**wachtel** *(Ger.)* quail call
**wada** *(Chile)* maracas
**waldteufel** *(Ger.)* friction drum
**walzentrommel** *(Ger.)* cylindrical drum
**waschbrett** *(Ger.)* washboard
**wellensirene** *(Ger.)* siren
**werbel** *(Pol.)* drum
**wewetl** *(Mex. Ind.)* a large ornately covered single headed wooden drum
**windmaschine** *(Ger.)* wind machine
**wirbeltrommel** *(Ger.)* tenor drum
**woda** *(L. Amer.)* maracas

# X

**xaqué-xaqué** *(Braz.)* a double rattle on a stick
**xere** *(Port.)* samba shaker
**xilofon** *(Sp.)* xylophone
**xilofono** *(It.)* xylophone
**xilofono a tastiera** *(It.)* keyboard xylophone
**xilofono basso** *(It.)* bass xylophone
**xilofono in cassetta di risonanza** *(It.)* trough xylophone
**xilomarimba** *(It.)* xylomarimba
**xilomarimbe** *(It.)* xylomarimba
**xilophon basso** *(It.)* bass xylophone
**xilorgano** *(Sp.)* xylophone
**xocalho** *(L. Amer.)* metal tube shaker
**xucalho** *(L. Amer.)* metal tube shaker

**xucalhos de metal** *(L. Amer.)* metal tube shaker
**xulonphone** *(Gr.)* xylophone
**xylofono** *(It., Sp.)* xylophone
**xylophon** *(Ger., Fr.)* xylophone
**xylophone à cassette resonance** *(Fr.)* trough xylophone
**xylophone à clavier** *(Fr.)* keyboard xylophone
**xylophone basse** *(Fr.)* bass xylophone
**xylosistron** *(Ger.)* xylophone

# Y

**yuka** *(L. Amer.)* a single headed conga type drum
**yunque** *(Sp.)* anvil

# Z

**zacapa** *(Andean)* an Andean jingle rattle
**zacatán** *(Mayan)* a large ornately covered single headed
    wooden drum
**zapotecano**...marimba
**ziehpfeife** *(Ger.)* slide whistle
**zilafone** *(It.)* xylophone
**zilafono** *(It.)* xylophone
**zilia** *(Ger.)* small pair of cymbals
**zimbel** *(Ger.)* antique cymbal
**zimbeln** *(Ger.)* antique cymbals
**zimbelrad** *(Ger.)* bell wheel
**zimbelstern** *(Ger.)* bell wheel
**zumbidor** *(Braz.)* bull roarer or thunder stick
**zumbumba** *(Port.)* lion's roar
**zusam** *(Ger.)* crash cymbals
**zuzá** *(Braz.)* metal tube shaker
**zylindertrommeln** *(Ger.)* cylindrical drums

# BIBLIOGRAPHY

Apel, Willi. *Harvard Dictionary of Music.* Second Edition. Cambridge, Mass.: The Belknap Press of Harvard University Press, 1972.

Betteridge, Harold T., ed. *The New Cassel's German Dictionary.* New York: Funk & Wagnalls, Co., Inc., 1958.

Blades, James. *Percussion Instruments and Their History.* London: Faber & Faber, 1970.

Blatter, Alfred. *Instrumentation/Orchestration.* New York: Longman Inc., 1980.

Blom, Eric. *Grove's Dictionary of Music and Musicians.* Vol. 1-10, Fifth Edition. New York: St. Martin's Press Inc., 1954.

Brindle, Reginald Smith. *Contemporary Percussion.* London: Oxford University Press, 1975.

Carroll Sound Incorporated. *CARROLL SOUNDS GALLERY SOUND* catalog. New York, N.Y.:

Combs, Michael F. *Percussion Manual.* Belmont, California: Wadsworth Publishing Co., Inc., 1977.

Diagram Group. *Musical Instruments of the World.* Holland: Diagram Visual Information Ltd., 1976.

The Dudenredaktion and The German Section of The Oxford University Press Dictionary Department, ed. The Oxford-Duden Pictorial German-English Dictionary. Oxford: Clarendon Press, 1980.

Firth, Vic. *Percussion Symposium.* New York: Carl Fisher, Inc., 1966.

Forsyth, Cecil. *Orchestration.* London: Macmillan & Co., Limited & Strainer & Bell, Limited, 1929.

Holland, James. *Percussion.* New York, N.Y.: Macmillan Publishing Co., Inc., 1978.

Kennan, Kent Wheeler. *The Technique of Orchestration.* Englewood Cliffs, N.J.: Prentice-Hall, Inc., 1970.

Lang, Morris, and Larry Spivack. *Dictionary of Percussion Terms.* New York: Lang Percussion Co., 1977.

Latin Percussion Catalog. Third Edition. Garfield, N.J.: Latin Percussion Inc., 1981.

Marcuse, Sibyl. *A Survey of Musical Instruments.* New York, N.Y.: Harper & Row Publishing, Inc., 1975.

Marcuse, Sibyl. *Musical Instruments, A Comprehensive Dictionary.* Garden City, N.Y.: Doubleday & Co., Inc., 1964.

Payson, Al and Jack McKenzie. *Percussion In The School Music Program.* Park Ridge, Illinois: Payson Percussion Products, 1976.

Peinkofer, Karl, and Fritz Tannigel. *Handbook of Percussion Instruments.* N.Y.: Belwin-Mills Publishing Corp., 1969.

Piston, Walter. *Orchestration.* N.Y.: W. W. Norton & Co., Inc., 1955.

Reynolds, Barbra. ed. *The Cambridge Italian Dictionary.* Great Britain: Cambridge University Press, 1962.

Richards, Emil. *Range Finder For The "Percussion" Seeker.* 5173 Santa Monica Blvd., Hollywood, California: 1977.

Rosen, Michael,. "Terms Used In Percussion." *Percussive Notes,* Vol. 13-16, 18-19.

Sachs, Curt. *The History of Musical Instruments.* New York: W. W. Norton & Co., Inc., 1940.

Scholes, Percy A. *The Oxford Companion To Music.* Ninth Edition. London: Oxford University Press, 1955.

Slonimsky, Nicholas. *Music of Latin America.* New York: Da Capo Press, 1972.

White, Charles L. *Drums Through The Ages.* Los Angeles, California: The Sterling Press, 1960.